A GHOST COMES
CALLING

An adoptee's journey to understand the sister she never knew

REBECCA TITCHNER

SUNBURY
P R E S S ®
Mechanicsburg, PA USA

Published by Sunbury Press, Inc.
Mechanicsburg, PA USA

SUNBURY
P R E S S
www.sunburypress.com

For information about special discounts for bulk purchases, please contact Sunbury Press Orders Dept. at (855) 338-8359 or orders@sunburypress.com.

To request one of our authors for speaking engagements or book signings, please contact Sunbury Press Publicity Dept. at publicity@sunburypress.com.

FIRST SUNBURY PRESS EDITION: July 2024

Set in Adobe Garamond Pro | Interior design by Crystal Devine | Cover by Mark Cela | Edited by Sarah Peachey.

Publisher's Cataloging-in-Publication Data
Names: Titchner, Rebecca, author.
Title: A ghost comes calling : an adoptee's journey to understanding the sister she never knew / Rebecca Titchner.
Description: First trade paperback edition. | Mechanicsburg, PA : Sunbury Press, 2024.
Summary: Is it possible to know someone from only the words they've left behind? Rebecca Titchner pieces her sister's life together from two decades of journals in an adoption memoir that takes the reader on a journey through both their lives and her sister's tragic death.
Identifiers: ISBN : 979-8-88819-236-8 (paperback) | ISBN : 979-8-88819-237-5 (ePub).
Subjects: FAMILY & RELATIONSHIPS / Siblings | FAMILY & RELATIONSHIPS / Adoption & Fostering | TRUE CRIME / Murder / General.

Designed in the USA
0 1 1 2 3 5 8 13 21 34 55

For the Love of Books!

For Frances and Dana, I wish we would have had more time.
For my nieces, I wish I could have made a difference.

~~⚬✾⚬~~

CONTENTS

Foreword by Mark Cela | *vii*

Author's Note | *xi*

CHAPTERS

1. Wanted. Special. Chosen. 1
2. Wednesday's Child is Full of Woe 10
3. My Daily Journal 14
4. Darkness Around the Edges 18
5. Finery and a Fickle Heart 21
6. We've Only Just Begun 30
7. A Wagon Full of Heartache 41
8. Setting the Stage for Change 48
9. Harbinger 52
10. My Orphan Soul 55
11. Pretty Polly 60
12. This Love Will Never Save You 69
13. Perfect Strangers 77
14. Flesh For Fantasy 81
15. Coup 84
16. Finding My Way Home 91
17. Motherless Child 102
18. Tired of Running 107

19. Through the Eyes of a Child   113

20. The Cost of Freedom   116

21. The Grass is Always Greener   126

22. An Orphan Again   133

23. No Such Thing as Enough   138

24. Hatred and Heartache   142

25. I'm Death, I Come to Take the Soul, Leave
     the Body and Leave it Cold   148

26. 30 x 16.5 x 15.5   151

27. The Missing Piece   154

28. Who am I, Really?   158

29. A Ghost Comes Calling   164

Epilogue: September 2023 Full Circle | 172

Acknowledgments | 175

About the Author | 176

FOREWORD

By Mark Cela

I consider my experience in this story to be quite rare. I am a brother of two sisters who both knew me, but who never met one another. They knew each existed, and both knew their mother, but neither sister had spoken or corresponded with the other while both were alive. Bekki, the author of this book, began a relationship with her sister Dana through reading Dana's lifelong personal journals. Dana had not given these journals to Bekki, rather Bekki acquired them after Dana died.

It sounds like the beginning of a fantastic story, right?

The journals that inspired this book carry with them a fascinating story beyond the one written inside their pages. To be completely transparent, I haven't read the journals and probably never will. I don't feel it's my place to read them. When I was in my late teens, Dana asked me, if she were to die unexpectedly, what was the one thing of hers I wanted. I said the journals. They were the body of work she produced that had the most profound meaning to her. Since that conversation years ago, much has happened, and I am happy for Bekki to own them. I was fortunate to have a relationship with Dana, something Bekki never got to have. She has developed a unique understanding of Dana through the journals that I feel give her the right to own them.

Through various conversations over the years, Dana told me the journals were written in three different forms. Some passages were an accurate recounting of her feelings and observations throughout her life. Others were a more stylized and romantic version of events. A few were fiction, writing that was purposefully included to infuriate those who read her journals without her consent. If her husband was accusing her of an affair she never actually had, never verbally mentioned, but had written about in the journals, she knew he had been invading her privacy. It was a brilliant approach that caused her more than a few arguments over the course of her life.

Outside of the journals, Dana wrote dozens of fictional short stories, biographies, and several screenplays. The fiction was loosely inspired by a hodgepodge of real events, but as Dana would admit, in the end they were highly dramatized fictional stories. As you'll read in this book, there is a key point in Dana's life when she moved to New Orleans. This is about the time I began to lose contact with her. In recent years I've read the accounts of people in New Orleans who knew her. Several people recounted stories of Dana's origins before New Orleans. The stories were familiar but not accurate to her life story. I later realized where I heard the origin stories before. These were events she had written in a screenplay nearly a decade earlier. Dana had been living in New Orleans as one of her characters.

She began slowly changing herself about a year before she left her family. Dana thought her laugh was awful, so she changed it. She changed her mannerisms. She changed the way she walked. She began telling people about events in her life that were completely based on what she had written in various stories. At one point, her husband told me he didn't know what reality was to Dana anymore. She moved to New Orleans, where no one knew her, and became the character she had loosely written in a screenplay as an avatar of herself, Polly.

Dana was my best friend growing up. She was a wonderful sister, old enough to give life advice but young enough that I would listen and not dismiss it as nagging. She was funny and full of life but had an unfortunately strong streak of low self-esteem, something that would eventually consume her. She was at constant odds with our mother, someone who shared many of the same harmful traits. Both were from a long line of women with anger and depression issues, each generation hating the one before for not possessing the self-awareness to stop the cycle.

Dana and I began hearing rumors of Bekki when we were kids. Bekki was this mysterious child who had supposedly been given up for adoption after a scandalous affair my mother had in her late teens. She was the skeleton in Mom's closet no one mentioned but who everyone clearly knew existed. I was in my mid-twenties when I finally met Bekki, and where Dana was so much like our mother, Bekki was just like me. There was no real awkwardness between us; it was immediately apparent she was my sister, and she has been treated as such ever since.

At the time I met Bekki, Dana had moved to New Orleans and began a new life there. She refused to meet Bekki. The few times I spoke to Dana after her move, and the last time she visited, she was no longer the sister I knew. I told her she was heading down a path I refused to follow. That argument was the last time I saw her alive.

What Bekki has compiled in this book is nothing short of a profound letter from one sister to another. It's an examination of one sister searching for her natural family while the other did everything she could to escape it. I have great respect for what Bekki has created in this book, and I am proud to have been a reference for the creation. While Dana was our sister, this book is Bekki and Dana's story.

AUTHOR'S NOTE

Dana's journals turned up many years after I located my birth family, and I was beyond fortunate to be given them for safekeeping. Dana had written many times that her journals would be her legacy, and I expect that she believed they would provide a measure of celebrity, the one thing she desperately wanted. Ironically, it was me, the sister she never knew, who put Dana's words into the world so that she isn't forgotten.

All journal entries, letters, and notes appear in their original form.

"It's no use going back to yesterday, because I was
a different person then."

—Lewis Carroll, *Alice's Adventures in Wonderland*

Not long after Hurricane Katrina in late August 2005, Dana Pastori's mother posted on a missing persons board, seeking information on Dana's whereabouts.

She hadn't spoken to her daughter since 1996.

Her plea would go unanswered.

This is a story about my sister:
A person I never knew.
I conjured her life from her words.
This is a story about me and our parallel lives.
This is a story about adoption.

CHAPTER 1

WANTED. SPECIAL. CHOSEN.

On September 13, 1960, an unwed nineteen-year-old gave birth to a five-pound baby girl at Hamot Hospital in Erie, Pennsylvania. That infant was immediately placed for adoption.

The day I turned thirty-six was the day I found out I was born at 7 A.M. My adoptive parents never really talked about my actual birth because they weren't there. Nor did they know anything about the young woman who brought me into the world. Did she have a difficult pregnancy? Was it a hard labor? What was she like? What were the circumstances of her life? The answers to these questions, and perhaps many others, weren't something they wanted or needed to know. It would be best if my story began in late autumn when they walked through the door of their home with a very tiny baby girl in their arms.

Knowing the time I was born changed something in me; it was as though before that moment I wasn't quite corporeal. It was a small thing, but to me it was powerful. It was the first step to an identity. I finally had a real name and a real mother and, most importantly to me, a real beginning.

I located my birth mother, Frances, in March 1996, six months before my thirty-sixth birthday.

On that particular day, six months after I had first heard her voice, my birth mother called me at 7 A.M., said good morning, wished me a happy birthday, and then said this: "And this is when you were born."

We were still in a honeymoon phase of our relationship, my birth mom and me, and she sent me roses that year—thirty-six roses, one for each year—and a card. Inside the card, she wrote:

Bekki, may I send you a hundred of these. I missed so many of your birthdays. But in my heart and the hidden recesses of my mind I never forgot a one. I love you my daughter. This year is the best of all. You are in it, you are finally in my life. We'll be together soon to talk and laugh and get to know one another even more. I'm so proud of you! See you soon. Oxoxox

<hr />

The story of my birth began one night in December 1959.

Frances, then eighteen, was a waitress in a jazz nightclub in Niagara Falls, New York, called The Ontario House. The club, located on Ontario near Main Street, was iconic in the 1940s and '50s, and in the world of jazz, it was legendary. For many years it was *the* place to hear jazz in the Niagara Falls region.

An amazing number of musicians from Western New York made it to the big time, and many of them had their start at the Ontario House, or "the O-H," as it was called. Studio guitarist Tommy Tedesco started there. Jazz saxophonist John "Spider" Martin, who went on to perform with artists such as Aretha Franklin, Etta James, and Tony Bennett, also performed there. Often, when Martin returned to Niagara Falls, it was not uncommon that he brought musicians like Dizzy Gillespie and Lee Konitz with him.

The late Richard Kermode was a teenager when he began playing keyboards in a jazz group at the Ontario House. He would later play with rock greats Janis Joplin and Santana, among others.

The club hosted a virtual Who's Who of jazz during its heyday. Dizzy Gillespie, Maynard Ferguson, Chuck Mangione, and others came by after their gigs elsewhere in the area to listen and sometimes sit in. One night Johnny Cash stopped by after his gig and spent the remainder of the evening at the end of the bar talking to patrons and listening to whoever was on the bill that night.

The Ontario House in Niagara Falls, New York. Frances worked as a waitress there, and this is where she met my birth father.

Venues like the Ontario House held a certain mystique, and Frances was swept up by its magic.

It was almost Christmas. It was after-hours. She was infatuated with the owner of the place, a mountain of a man who loved good cigars, good liquor, jazz music, and beautiful women. He had been called back home when he was a sophomore at the Pratt Institute in New York City to take over the family business. He was estranged from his wife and had three young daughters.

Frances drank whisky while he sipped cognac, and painted.

The owner was my birth father.

Frances said she got pregnant the first time they had sex. During the hundreds of conversations we had over the years, I never asked her about the fallout. Whom did she confide in? Did she ever even consider keeping me? Did she even have a say in the matter?

A few months into her pregnancy, Frances left Niagara Falls to "visit family." That was the official story. In reality she was sent to the Florence Crittenton Home for Unwed Mothers in Erie. There, she would serve out her penance as an unmarried pregnant teen, give up the baby, whom she named Marie Bernadette Scott, and then move on with her life.

These homes were a far cry from the purpose of the first Florence Crittenton Home, the Florence Night Mission, which opened in 1883 on New York City's Bleeker Street. Its goals were to reform so-called "fallen" women as well as provide shelter for unmarried pregnant women and girls.

Charles Nelson Crittenton, a wealthy New York businessman, established the first home in memory of his daughter, Florence, who died at age four. With its success, Crittenton became a traveling evangelist, preaching, in particular, to prostitutes and unwed mothers. By 1892, Crittenton Homes were established throughout the US.

By the early 1900s, the primary focus of the National Florence Crittenton Mission was the rescue and care of unwed mothers, their need for adequate medical care, and their right to raise their children free from the scorn of society. According to a Virginia Commonwealth University publication on the history of these homes, "Except in extreme circumstances, Crittenton policy opposed the separation of mother and child for adoption and believed that children should be kept out of institutions. In fact, motherhood was seen as a means of reform and the Crittenton home as a training ground for responsible motherhood and self-support."

This policy changed drastically during the Baby Scoop Era, the years 1945–1973, when more than 1.5 million pregnant girls and women in the U.S. were sent away to maternity homes to surrender children in secret. By the 1960s, over two hundred homes for unmarried pregnant women were operating across forty-four states, including Pennsylvania. Daughters were sent away to these homes to wait out their pregnancies and relinquish their babies to married couples who could raise them without the stigma and shame of illegitimacy.

My birth mother was among them.

Frances was always reluctant to talk to me about those few months when she was in a place with other women who were brought together for the sole purpose of having a baby and walking away. The goal was to forget. She was to forget about the child she carried for nine months, forget about the fate of this child, and forget that she was even a mother.

She said that she refused to sign the relinquishment papers until they allowed her to hold me. She also said she had a photo of me as a newborn, which, apparently, was lost over the years. Whether these two things are true, I'll never know. Nor will I know who took her there—her mother couldn't drive—or who picked her up and what the conversation entailed during the trip home. Or maybe she was forced to take a bus. I don't know which situation would have been worse.

Frances once told me that my great aunts always hoped that I would someday show up at one of their homes in Niagara Falls, searching for my mother. How ironic that they wanted me to find my way back but that no one wanted to keep me.

I was taken to an orphanage called St. Joseph's Home for Children in Erie, and an organization called Catholic Social Services (now Catholic Charities) handled my eventual adoption. Frances went back to Niagara Falls, where she promptly enlisted in the navy.

In late October 1960, I was adopted by a couple nearly old enough to be my birth mother's parents. They lived in a small town in Elk County, about 120 miles southeast of Erie, and in the fifteen years that they had been married, they weren't able to have children.

I heard a story once from a friend of the family, not long after I had found Frances, that my parents had adopted a baby before me, but that the birth mother changed her mind and they had to give the baby back. I also heard from this same person that my adoptive mother had a false pregnancy, clinically termed *pseudocyesis*. She believed she was expecting a baby—she looked pregnant—but was not really carrying a child.

In a letter from the Diocese of Erie's Department of Charities dated June 24, 1958, my adoptive parents were told: "We have received your completed adoption application. It will be put on file with our long waiting list, as you know; but we will contact you as soon as we are able to give your application active consideration."

Not long after giving me up for adoption Frances joined the navy.

In 1960, their dream of having a family became a reality when they adopted me. My dad often told me that he wanted a little girl. I'm not sure whether I ever believed it, but I suppose it was his way of telling me that I was wanted, special, and chosen. These are the three words most often used in adoption, as though somehow the child was saved from a certain cruel fate. The truth was this: My parents couldn't have a baby, and I was available. Both nearing forty, they must have felt this was their last chance.

On the way back from Erie—my adoptive mom's sister made the trip with them, and she told me this story—they had to stop at a little motel about an hour north of their home. This particular aunt was one of my favorites, and she loved recalling the story to me. She said I was fussy in the car and most likely hungry. It was a cold night, and they all thought

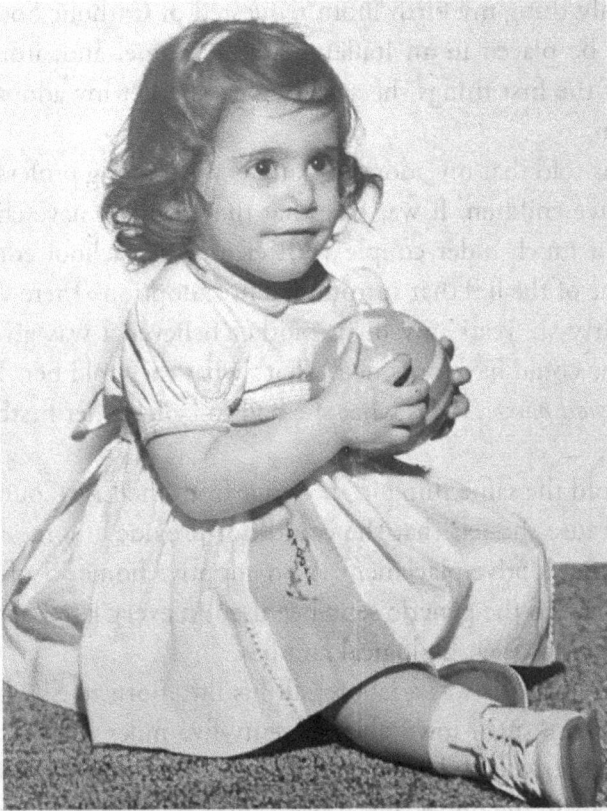

There are very few photos of me as an infant/toddler. This photo is most likely mid-1961.

that the remainder of the trip would be much better for everyone if I was fed, so they asked someone at the front desk to warm up a bottle for me.

Did anyone ask about the baby in the car? Did the person at the desk wonder whether the baby was someone's grandchild? Did my adoptive mom hang on to me tight, afraid that the young woman who was somewhere out there might want me back? The thoughts of losing another child to a birth mother who wanted her baby back had to weigh heavily on her. This baby was going to be hers, and no one was going to take it away.

That place where they stopped is still standing, but the little cottages are now run-down efficiency apartments and dilapidated storage units. Sometimes I try to envision the warm glow of little, tidy, freshly painted buildings welcoming travelers on a long trip or perhaps welcoming a baby in a car with three strangers on her way to a new life.

The only thing my birth mom requested of Catholic Social Services was that I be placed in an Italian-Catholic home, and, ironically, that was one of the first things she asked me—whether my adoptive parents were Italian.

She was told that my adoptive parents were young professionals who couldn't have children. It was true that they couldn't have children, but they were a much older couple with elementary school educations. It was just one of the lies that surrounded my adoption. There were others, but for thirty-six years, my birth mother believed I was given a better life than she could have provided. That's what they told her. *Your baby is going to a good home.* That's what she had to believe: her firstborn would be all right.

I was told the same thing in the letter from the Erie County court in 1993: "Because she felt that she could not provide a home for you she requested an adoptive placement in an adoptive home." I often wonder whether that was the generic sentence used in every letter sent to adoptees searching for their biological families.

My adoptive dad was a laborer all his life. Born to Southern Italian immigrants in a small town about twenty-five miles from where I grew up, he worked in the coal mines and then in a factory. He had Black Lung from his years in the mines, but it was cancer that finally killed him.

He once told me that he met my adoptive mom one evening when he was out with his friends and, that same night, announced that he would someday marry her. She came from a large family and her father worked on the railroad, though rumor also had it that he engaged in some moonshining on the side. They owned a decent piece of property and kept livestock for butchering. My adoptive mom worked in factories during World War II, but for most of her adult life she was a housewife. She also suffered from mental illness. When she was in her late seventies, she had a psychotic break while residing at an assisted-living facility and was sent to an inpatient geriatric psychiatric unit, but she struggled her entire life. She heard voices, she believed that people were always talking about her, and she thought strangers were outside our home at night. Many members of her family had been hospitalized for mental health problems either locally or in state hospitals. This was the woman who was to be my mother.

These were my beginnings. I was a sickly child and the local doctor made many late-night house calls to my home. I was afraid to walk on the grass. I often fell asleep on my adoptive father's chest because he was warm and I was always cold.

My adoptive parents in 1945.

CHAPTER 2

WEDNESDAY'S CHILD IS FULL OF WOE

Frances delivered her second child, also a girl, in Corpus Christi, Texas, on Wednesday, August 7, 1963.

My birth mother, fresh from the trauma of giving up her firstborn, began a new life by enlisting in the navy. But it was not the life she envisioned.

In 1963, Frances had a second child, Dana Marie—her middle name chosen because it was my first. Dana was not given up for adoption.

In a time when unwed mothers rarely kept their babies, my birth mother held tight to her second-born. Perhaps it was because her mother no longer controlled her life or because she was in the navy and so far away; it was easier to create a fictional story surrounding Dana's birth. Or maybe the real reason was because she couldn't bear losing another child.

My mother was head over heels for Dana's father—a fellow serviceman—even though he was married with a family of his own.

When I first found Frances, we talked as much about Dana as we did my life. I remember sitting on the steps of my front porch, listening to her reminisce about her time in the navy. She told me she had no idea Dana's father was married. A fellow WAVE warned her about him, telling Frances that, in fact, he was married with children and that she should break off the relationship. Frances insisted she tried but that he continued to pursue her. He had no intention of leaving his family for Frances. She was pregnant and all alone for the second time.

Frances raised Dana as a single parent. Several years later, after many moves and many jobs, she married and had one more child, my brother, Mark. Mark's dad, Frank, was a tool and die maker, and the couple eventually settled in the Dayton, Ohio, area.

Mark, eleven years my junior, grew up with Dana. Of all the people who passed through her tumultuous life, he undoubtedly knew her the best. According to Mark, Dana was fun and intelligent, but he added, "I can't say she was kind." Empathy, apparently, was not a word he ever used to describe our sister.

That said, he remembered what a great "big sister" she was to him when he was growing up. "She loved family," Mark told me. He said that she wanted to be a positive influence in his life.

All that would eventually change.

When I first began reading Dana's journals, I asked Mark if he could tell me more about my sister. In all the years he and I had known one another, I never asked him who Dana was as a person. This was his list of recollections:

She loved calligraphy.
She was a great cook.
She had a pen pal in the Philippines.
She loved Frank Herbert's *Dune, The Lord of the Rings*, and the *Xanth* novels.
She loved the PBS *Poldark* series and Rankin and Bass's *The Hobbit*.
She watched *Rudolph the Red-Nosed Reindeer* and *Charlie Brown* holiday specials every year.
She also loved *Monty Python* and *Star Wars*.
She liked video games, especially role-playing ones.
She liked all kinds of music, not just Led Zeppelin. No country, though.
She used to wear a black leather jacket.
She once permed her hair so badly that Mom let her stay home from school.

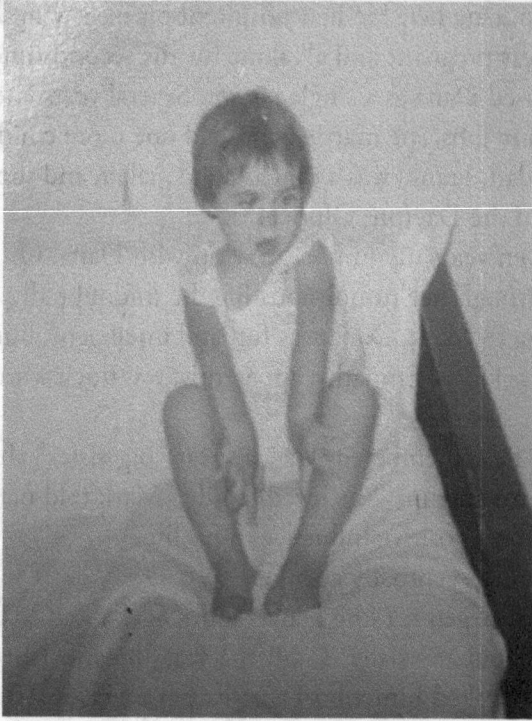

A very young Dana.

I never knew my sister Dana and yet, I am compelled to somehow understand who she was.

Maybe, I thought, by understanding her, I would begin to understand myself and the blood that connected us to each other and to our mother.

No more than a month after I found Frances in March 1996, Dana severed all ties with her family. What appeared to me to be a disagreement between Frances and Dana was actually the end of their relationship. Their estrangement was permanent and its effects far-reaching. I was unwittingly immersed in an unraveling family tragedy, one that had a huge impact on my relationship with my birth mother.

Frances and I talked regularly, sometimes for hours. While I don't remember the details of most of these conversations, there was one particular call that I can still envision vividly, even decades after it happened.

It was April 1996, on or very near my birth mom's birthday. I was sitting on an overstuffed chair in the corner of my living room, listening, with disbelief, to the things Frances told me, and, for a fleeting moment, I wondered whether I would regret searching for my birth family. My sister, along with her new boyfriend, had essentially kidnapped her own daughters and was on the run. Frances talked to her on the phone but told me she didn't know where she was. Dana was a fugitive, and her ex-husband wanted her arrested and their two daughters removed from her care.

Frances said she told Dana about me and that Dana responded, "It looks like you found one daughter and lost another." I didn't really know how to take her comment. It had an unsettling sting to it. Dana was just told by Frances that she had another sister, and that fact seemed to mean absolutely nothing to her.

What I didn't know was the backstory, and I wouldn't find out this story until I read Dana's journals.

During the phone call, Dana and Frances argued over the $6,000-plus charges on Frances's credit card. It wasn't so much the charges as what some of them were: high-end lingerie and expensive clothes. Frances was so mad that she told Dana, "You are dead to me."

This was the last conversation they ever had, and the final time Frances would hear her daughter's voice. Those five words, spoken in anger in the heat of the moment, couldn't be taken back. What I also didn't know—and what Frances never knew—was it wouldn't have really mattered. Dana was already long gone.

It wasn't what Frances said. Dana and Frances had always had an uneasy relationship. My brother told me more than once that Dana was terrified of Frances. And yet, of her three children, Dana was the child she cherished most. This fact wasn't lost on Dana and she used it to her advantage, borrowing money many times, from not only her mother, but her grandmother, aunt, and in-laws as well.

There were plenty of journal entries in which Dana wrote about her frustration and anger with her mother. So Frances telling Dana that she was dead to her wasn't something Dana would take to heart for long.

It was something else completely, this fatal detail. It was the one thing that had enough sway and power over Dana to convince her that closing the door on her family forever was the best thing she could do.

It was her new boyfriend.

CHAPTER 3

MY DAILY JOURNAL

Dana and I both kept journals when we were young. My journaling would become sporadic as I got older, but she faithfully kept a journal for over twenty years.

I became acquainted with Dana through her many journals, spanning the years 1979–2001. The fact that two decades of journals survived her many moves and life changes was amazing in itself.

I really didn't know what to expect when I opened the first one in the autumn of 2018. I honestly didn't think we would be anything alike. Still, as I read through the pages, I realized the parallels of our lives were eerily similar. This particular version of Dana was not unlike me and what I wrote about my life. What was written wasn't necessarily absolute truth. If anything, the journals offered a glimpse at what lies beneath.

Dana began her first journal on Christmas Day, 1979. It was a small, off-white book the size of a diary, with a lock and the words "My Daily Journal" etched in a metallic magenta script, surrounded by tendrils and flowers and a butterfly. I expect it was a gift from our mother. Frances told me many times how much Dana loved to write.

"*You must see that I learn and always teach me,*" she told this new but constant companion. She was sixteen-and-a-half years old and life was full of promise.

"*I am at peace and excited for a bright future,*" she wrote shortly after New Year's Day 1980.

The journal would become a confidante. It shared all of her struggles. It became the only perpetual thing in her life.

In many ways, Dana was a typical teenager. She worried about her looks and was crazy about this boy or that one, in particular one named Jim. Even then, she wrote about finding her knight in shining armor. She was a voracious reader and was drawn to literature and movies about England and Scotland.

Wildly romantic, Dana wrote about the characters she encountered as if they were old friends. In fact, these literary personas made up most of the entries in her first journal. She took on the pen name of Katherine Swynford, the Duchess of Lancaster, and would sign each entry "Katherine" instead of "Dana." Interestingly enough, in the notes highlighting a biography of Swynford, written by author Alison Weir, *Mistress of the Monarchy*, Swynford was considered a woman ahead of her time, a woman who made her own choices and took control of her own destiny. Weir believed that without Swynford, the course of English history would have been much different.

These were also Dana's aspirations when she was seventeen. She was headstrong, outspoken, and determined to be successful and independent. On March 10, 1980, she wrote, *"Yet I ask, am I worthy of the Katherine name—should I not choose another—within—yet to separate myself and keep reality. I'll think on it. 1-2-3!!"* She would often write of how she must travel to the places that captured her imagination: England, Scotland, and Cornwall. At this time in her life, she had one foot planted in Ohio and the other far across the Atlantic.

"It would make no difference how many hours I laid awake—I am in most pleasing spirits!" Dana wrote on November 28, 1980. *"My destiny I'm sure lies in England! Whether it is on the stage or in the midst of rural cultural society the matter would mean little to me."*

In January 1977, when I was nearly sixteen-and-a-half years old, I, too, started a journal. Mine was a three-ring binder covered in blue denim cloth, and it was divided into sections. There was Daily Log, Dialogue with Persons, Dialogue with Society, Dialogue with Body, Dream Log, and others. Unlike Dana's early entries, mine were extensive, rambling missives. I wrote of not only what was going on inside my head, but

Undated photo of teenage Dana.

my day-to-day life. School. Band. Parties. Boys. And I wrote something nearly every day.

But certainly, I sounded like a teenager, full of angst at times and unsure of the future or my place in the world. Self-discovery was a messy thing. During my junior and senior years in high school, these were my challenges:

> January 13, 1977: "*Today may be a very important stepping stone in my life. I've discovered something of which I never knew existed in me. The capacity to love myself . . . to be happy is all I seek.*"
>
> February 6, 1977: "*I'm scared. I'm insecure. I'm lonely.*"
>
> January 30, 1977: "*I'm fighting to keep away from food.*"

March 7, 1977: *"Will people ever notice me? Why is it that my girl-friends get all the dates and I end up sitting home?"*
December 12, 1977: *"We create images to others, and come to believe those images as being us."*

I read, too. It was an escape, a way to leave the room and the house and the life I inhabited. But while Dana was enamored with romance, I preferred books that were much darker and erotic. My parents would have been horrified to know what I was reading each night. *The Exorcist. Fear of Flying. 9 1/2 Weeks.* Anais Nin. The closest library to where I grew up was twelve miles away, so I would use the money I had from doing odd jobs to order most of them. I bought *The Exorcist* at a local store and hid it until I got home. After I read it, several of my classmates borrowed it, hiding it from their parents, too, I'm sure. By the time it was eventually returned to me, it was in tatters. My parents both read the evening paper and the *TV Guide*, but I don't recall either of them ever reading a book.

CHAPTER 4

DARKNESS AROUND THE EDGES

Dana and I had never met, but we were each drawn to that which was bad for us, both physically and emotionally.

Even as a teenager, Dana began to embrace a darkness that eventually would define her. She was always inventing and reinventing herself, and she often penned that she was lonely and restless but thrived on the melancholy. She was bored with the "*norm*," as she once wrote, and she strongly believed she had a destiny with someone. This belief—and it carried through her whole life—would be her undoing.

"*Kevin, Mike, Jim, Jim, Larry. They are all part of my picture. Yet none stands out—he is prophesied to come later,*" she wrote on March 26, 1980. Dana never explained where this prophecy originated; it always seemed to be there. One thing was for certain: She believed it without question.

I looked at life completely differently and with much less romance and mystery. The summer of my seventeenth year, I wrote, "*I'm searching for the perfect guy. Needless to say, I'll never have him.*" I never believed I deserved to be happy, or that I really deserved anything.

———⌘———

Dana, on the other hand, believed she was owed the world.

Two lifelong issues had their beginnings in the first pages of that original journal: an obsession over her weight and a desire for security, to be pampered, adored. In particular, she yearned for the romance of being swept off her feet and embraced in a loving, unending relationship.

Her journal entries also revealed a strict and absolute schedule for everything in her life. Dieting. Writing. Reading. She told her journal: *"You shall be quite proud of my achievements in the end. I am sure I shall succeed!"*

My brother, Mark, said that Dana and Frances competed in the weight loss arena, taping photos of their backsides to the refrigerator door as an incentive. He told me the competition was fierce.

Dana's burden, or so she said, was her weight of 135, and she lamented that she was a *"slave to an ugly body and a cruel, non-under-standing world."* She wrote that her goal was 108 pounds, and she felt that if she attained that weight, her *"transformation"* to become a great beauty could begin. *"My absolute power and breeding and graces are apparent,"* she told her journal on July 13, 1980. This, too, would be a recurring theme throughout her life. The transformation to someone more refined, more educated, more eloquent, and always, always someone much thinner.

There were many promises to begin something "tomorrow." Tomorrow seemed to be a perfect day to start any change. She said it often and, almost always, never followed through.

She struggled to make friends and she wasn't a particularly good friend to those she had. The young woman who lived in a lush fantasy world of castles and heather was changing.

"I am no longer the daft child who rocks to and fro clutching books to win dreams," she revealed in the summer of 1981, not long before she turned eighteen. It was time to reinvent herself. *"I am a vixen and I lie very well."* The new Dana had arrived.

I never, for one moment, thought I was a vixen, but I was certainly aware of how I looked, and in my journals I would describe what I wore and how it made me feel.

In a journal entry on February 19, 1977, I described, in detail, the clothes I wore to go to a dance. I had a long, brown leather trench coat, and I loved how it could seemingly transform me. As for pants, the tighter, the better. I was deliberate in the outfits I chose and their impact not only on my psyche but how I appeared to others. Although reading these entries now makes me cringe just a little, I have always known that there is power in clothing, and so did Dana.

Beneath her leather jacket, keeping company with bad boys, and pushing every available envelope, Dana was a vulnerable young woman filled with self-loathing, and wanting, above anything else, to be famous.

~◆◆~

Like Dana, I craved attention, the dark ache of desire and being wanted. How many times was I in love? An embarrassing number. To me, love lost seemed the best kind. It was as though heartache was somehow better than a normal relationship. Or maybe I set myself up to lose on purpose, to feed the melancholy, to keep the game going on for as long as possible, and to be abandoned over and over and over. After all, that's how I began my life.

CHAPTER 5

FINERY AND A FICKLE HEART

Dana reveled in her high school graduation in 1981. I only felt sadness at mine. She spent her summer in love. I spent mine chasing after someone who didn't love me.

There was little mention of the events of Dana's senior year in this first journal. Much of her writing still revolved around literary characters, and she longed to be in England and Scotland. Her entries were heavy with flourish, and she called herself a *"creature of fire."*

In mid-September she wrote about being in love. *"A light streams through a window—a thought, a hope, a dream realized. My love again— again I bloom, again I am happy, but this time there is not that excitement, there is peace . . . sweet peace, why? Ask not . . ."*

The boy's name was Michael, and she called him a Christian and explained that they were going to the art museum together. *"I will be happy always,"* she wrote, even though she felt that he didn't love her as much as she loved him. She insisted that she wanted this relationship more than *"anything I can think of,"* but she left it in God's hands. By the beginning of 1981, Michael disappeared from her journals. She insisted that while they weren't compatible, she still loved him.

The holidays always meant a lot to Dana, and she seemed to find the time to write about them without fail, even when her life was at its lowest point. On November 23, 1980, she wrote, *"With the coming holidays I feel quite grand to say the least! A warmth for all and nostalgia lay in my heart!"*

She seemed happy and insisted in her entries that fame would be hers. She was looking forward to traveling to England after she graduated, and she reveled in what her future held. *"I am burning, alive with life . . . dreams of success, future, life . . . fantasies yet to be realized! Vixenry, chivalry, passion, lust, life!! It's all budding before me . . ."*

But there was no plan, at least none that she wrote in her journal. How would she manage to travel there? Who would pay for the trip? Would she go alone? What about college?

On May 3, 1981, she bought new clothes for graduation—*"finery,"* she called them—and graduated sixteen days later. *"I am happy to leave them all,"* she announced. *"This is what we all waited for—freedom and union. I feel magnificent! I am done and soon to begin. I am ecstatic! England soon!"*

Mark told me that high school wasn't easy for Dana. She felt awkward, like she didn't belong, and she had a real difficulty making friends. Although Dana had a way about her that drew people to her, she wasn't a popular girl.

I cataloged my senior year in painful detail. On January 1, 1978, I wrote: *"1978. I can't believe it's finally here. New Years Resolutions. Make National Honor Society. Find a job this summer. Make the Deans List in college. Better myself."* In reality I was already partying too much, and by the time I went to college, the dean's list was far from my mind.

When I look back, I realize that Dana and I were much alike in that neither of us felt we fit in, but while Dana's efforts to be a bad girl were mostly limited to the pages of her journal, I straddled two worlds. I was a National Honor Society student. I was also an out-of-control risk-taker and party girl.

I took my first drink at thirteen. I used to joke that by the time I was sixteen, I was really good at it. I found this in my high school journals, an entry from a party in December 1977:

> *In a circle, a dizzy maze. I'm smashed. Completely out of my mind. It's so hard to find myself because I don't know where I am . . . how did I manage to become like this? I'm fighting myself, someone I cannot overcome. I don't belong. My existence here isn't at all important to those whom I'm surrounded by. If I'm not drunk I'm high. It's so*

A photo from my junior year in high school, late 1976.

hard to be happy in a normal state of mind. I've got to learn to cope. The scapegoats run out. They don't last forever. I've run out of places to hide. As I sit here I wonder why the hell I'm sitting here writing all this. My mind is split. I am no longer one entity. It scares me. How can I let myself be this way? Where is my sensibility?

In a college journal, I found an entry discussing Walt Whitman's poem, "Song of Myself." In contrast, I penned this:

What is my song? Is it something I would want to sing out and let echo for everyone to hear or would I keep it hidden like a dirty

magazine or old love letters, damp and musty? What do I have
to sing? Do I have a song? Much of it was written in dark places,
laced with coke, pot, alcohol and anything else that would ease
pain. New—not new. There has been nothing new for a long time.
What do I need? Am I going crazy? I don't know where I belong.
My song . . . reaching for myself..I need to know me again, look in
the mirror and greet myself. Do you remember me, do you? Tell me,
please, tell me!

It would be years before my party was over. It would take until I was twenty-five and pregnant with my daughter. When Dana was twenty-five, her party was just beginning.

While Dana spent her senior year dreaming of a grand future somewhere in the UK, I spent my senior year in high school madly and stupidly in love with an older guy who lived four hours away. His family had a hunting camp in the area, and I met him at the little general store and gas station my dad's family owned. He was cute and funny and he had a really nice car.

In the days before the internet, cell phones, and instant gratification of text messaging, there were letters, expensive long-distance phone calls, and plenty of long, rambling journal entries about love, not to mention really bad love poems. I didn't see him often, which probably fueled the belief that absence made the heart grow fonder.

Looking back, I realize it was a strange relationship. Although I spent a dreadful amount of time obsessing over him, we never did more than kiss. He had a strange, erratic restlessness about him (which later I surmised may have been cocaine use), and I can't actually remember any really romantic moments, but I apparently felt as though he was the one.

My father liked him because he was an incredible athlete, a coal miner, and Italian. My mother liked him because he was kind to her. One thing for certain—he had old-school respect for his elders.

The low point of this relationship was when a friend of mine, feeling badly that I was hurting from not hearing from this guy, told me we could take his van and find him.

He lived in a small town in Fayette County, a nearly four-hour drive southwest of my home. We drove through Punxsutawney and Indiana,

Greensburg and Uniontown. We had a Pennsylvania road map but absolutely no idea where we were going. Of course, after hours and hours on the road, we gave up.

I can't remember why we never found his house. We wrote so many letters, so why didn't I have a street address? Or were the letters I sent him addressed to a post office box? Why didn't I ask someone? Why didn't I find a pay phone and call him? Or maybe the real reason was because he didn't want me to find him. Maybe, as Dana was apt to do, I created the entire relationship in my head. Sure, we had dates and saw each other when he came north to hunting camp, but I wasn't that naive. I had to know that he was most likely living a completely separate life, and that whoever he was involved with had no idea that when he traveled north with his friends to hunt and fish, he was seeing me.

I do remember the way I felt when we pulled into the driveway at my house. It was late—middle-of-the-night late. I was crushed. It felt like my world was crumbling. There I was, sitting in a van with a really great friend who would have done anything for me, who, for all I know, really loved me but was too insecure and shy to ask me out, and all I could do was whine about not finding my elusive boyfriend.

The trip was as futile as the relationship had been. It was time to move on. But I didn't. I hung on to this certainly failed relationship nearly through my entire freshman year at college, and I wrote about him obsessively in my journal. Dana and I were so much alike in this respect. Love was always entangled with obsession. Even though I was surrounded by a new group of friends, and even though there were several classmates who liked me and wanted to ask me out, I wallowed in the pitifulness of this relationship. I knew it was over, but I stubbornly refused to realize it. He wove in and out of my life for the next two years. This relationship was defined by an occasional phone call or letter and a couple visits to me at college. Just enough to never really allow me to forget him.

⁓⚬⚬⁓

My high school graduation finery was a white cotton dress printed with red roses bought from a clearance rack at Bloomingdale's while on a high school band trip to New York City.

Unlike Dana, I wasn't excited to graduate. I just wanted high school to be over. It was a beginning and an ending, and, in my world, there was nothing to celebrate. I don't recall my parents even taking my photo. A few of my parents' friends came to our house after graduation for a couple of drinks and some food, but there was no graduation party. Besides, I had to be up very early the next morning. The day after graduation I started a summer job to help pay for college. This job at a local grocery store was short-lived. The manager liked to harass the teenage girls that were hired in the summer. After a week of that, I quit and found another job. My dad's factory went on strike that summer, so lounging around until I left for college wasn't an option.

As a teenager, Dana had an enthusiasm and passion for life that I never did. My journal entries were never light or optimistic. I never dreamed. My biggest question to the universe was whether I would live to see twenty-one.

Dana spent her first days after graduation madly in love with a boy named Rich.

Her vision of love—the deep, deep need to be adored and the devastation of perceived rejection—would define every relationship she ever had. And it would be the fatal flaw of her last.

In her journal, May 25–28, 1981, she wrote:

"He called and he loves me. I love him."
"Richie loves me and I him. Parents are a problem to resolve. He is so
    beautiful and blonde."
"I have lost . . . he will not call because he has forgotten me."
"I do not trust him."
"He doesn't love me and did not think of me. I am sick inside and
    alone."

Dana's love affair with Rich was short-lived. The guy taking his place, a *"hot Sicilian,"* as she called him, would eventually become her husband. She lived and breathed being in love and enjoyed all the drama a new relationship brought. At nearly eighteen, it was a romance novel come to life, and she savored every minute.

I remember that kind of love very well. Heart-pounding, keep-you-awake-all-night, out-of-your-mind love. That was Dana. That was me. I was a serial offender; I was always in love.

On January 28, 1977, I pondered:

*Well, another day can be written off as history. It's a shame that
time travels so fast, especially when you want it to go slow and easy.
It seems the same for love. It's gone before one can take full hold and
hang on. Maybe it's meant to be that way; it keeps you searching and
chasing after it.*

Between early February and May 1977, my junior year in high
school, I was in love with at least three different guys. I lamented on
Valentine's Day that year that the holiday had come and gone. "*I checked
the mail today and there was nothing . . .*"

In mid-March, at a regional high school chorus festival, I met Steve,
who I described as having "black hair, piercing blue eyes, mustache . . . "
The dream guy I always wanted. I was enchanted. He played guitar and
had a beautiful tenor voice. "*He's only been gone for twenty minutes and
already I miss him*," I wrote in my journal after the festival was over.

By late April I was "*head over heels for him*," and we sent dozens of
letters to one another. He was even my date to the junior prom. But by
mid-May I was no longer in love with him; I was in love with someone
else.

So, when Dana wrote this on August 1, 1981, I could relate: "*I love
him and miss him and long for his touch. I would gladly bear his child,
marry him and live with him. Live somewhere in a fairy land.*"

With the "hot Sicilian" in her sights, Dana threw away Rich and, as
she was apt to do over and over, promptly fell in love.

But, as always, there was the trepidation that the decision she just
made would quash her "*dreams of grandeur.*" Or worse—that she really
wasn't in love, but simply looking for a way to escape that little farmhouse in Ohio.

I don't remember a time when I—just like Dana—didn't love to be
in love. I always ached to be touched. It always seemed that I, too, based
so many decisions on a lover. It became so much of a distraction that it
destroyed my life more than once. It erased opportunities and skewed
my focus. The schoolgirl crushes I wrote so much about when I was
sixteen and seventeen turned much darker as I got older. Boundaries

ceased to exist and there wasn't much I wouldn't do to chase down that thrill. I wouldn't stop, I couldn't stop, and although I wanted to change, I allowed myself to sink deep into the erotic but empty place that I loved and hated.

By the autumn of 1981, Dana was completely smitten with her new boyfriend. On November 19, 1981, she wrote,

> *Holidays are coming. Cold weather and warm fires. In this season I have someone to share with. In this—the happiest time of the year—I have someone who loves me. Someone to hold hands with, kiss under the mistletoe, love—So . . . I'm happy, gay, alive!*

Thanksgiving 1981 was as perfect as any holiday she would experience. Dana reveled in the holiday season, and having someone to love and who loved her must have thrilled her. *"Years from now I'll remember this holiday,"* she proclaimed on November 26. Her Thanksgiving was much different than my own that year.

While Dana was in Dayton, Ohio, celebrating Thanksgiving with her family and boyfriend, I was alone at Allegheny College, where I was finishing my senior year. I stayed at school during Thanksgiving break to study for a physics final rather than go home. I remember walking down the street toward town on Thanksgiving Day.

I was living off-campus in a two-bedroom apartment, and the student I shared the first-floor space with was gone for the weekend. By this time in my college career, I was ready to move on, but to what? The campus itself was beautiful, and Meadville wasn't much different than where I grew up, but I squandered opportunity there, too. All of that knowledge for the taking, and all I could do was think about the next party, the next guy, the next chance to melt into a smoky oblivion. One of my boyfriends loved the fact that I was not like the other girls at school. I didn't look like them and I didn't act like them. He meant it as a compliment, but to me, it meant four years of being an outsider. When I was young, I envisioned my time in college much differently. In a palette of autumn colors, I dreamed of walking down brick sidewalks wearing a wool blazer and skirt, books in hand, eager to learn and succeed. But that wasn't close to my reality.

I wasn't super smart. I wasn't pretty. I wasn't wealthy. I wasn't sorority material. I was the girl who didn't quite fit in. I was the girl who was laughed at and whispered about, someone on the outside, without a tribe. I was the girl who drank too much. I was the girl who was promiscuous. I was the girl you would fuck on a Saturday night but never bring home to your parents. They used to call it being from the wrong side of the tracks. I was that girl.

When I left my apartment, it was thirty-eight degrees and raining hard. I was wearing a pair of black jeans, a gray leather motorcycle jacket, and black boots. I don't recall where I was going. Nothing was open. Maybe I simply needed to walk, or maybe run away from something. Maybe that something was myself.

It was late afternoon, and the reflection of lights from houses glistened in puddles along the curb. People were gathered around tables, laughing, drinking, enjoying being together. I couldn't help but stare. It was every bit a Norman Rockwell print and it was everything that I didn't have.

I was lonely and I was angry and I knew that the phone call I hoped for wouldn't ever materialize. I spent part of the evening sitting on the cold wooden floor of the living room of my apartment with a bottle of wine listening to "Lover" by the Michael Stanley Band. True to form, there I was again, neck deep in the throes of unrequited love. For me, the holiday meal was compliments of Swanson, with a Jack Daniel's chaser.

CHAPTER 6

WE'VE ONLY JUST BEGUN

The idyllic lyrics of the Carpenters song "We've Only Just Begun" resonated with my teenage self. I truly believed this was how marriage should be. A lifelong partnership full of promise and unconditional love. Dana received an engagement ring four days before I was married in 1982; she married Frank nine months later.

Frank proposed on February 2, 1982, six months before Dana turned nineteen. In her journal, Dana wrote, *"Yesterday the Lord gave me a job and today he gave me a husband. Tonight he proposed."*

Later that week she vowed that she was *"determined to make him happy, happier than anyone else could make him . . . I just wish I had ample words to describe my feelings. I'm finally sure."*

On July 20, 1982, he bought her an engagement ring. She exclaimed that she was *"so in love!"* And in April 1983, they were married.

I imagine her wedding day, in early spring, when everything is a beautiful, lush green, and I smile at thinking of how much control Frances had to have of the entire event. And true to form, Mark told me that Frances's hat cost more than Dana's wedding dress.

I imagine brushing Dana's hair, maybe braiding it. I imagine putting flowers in her hair, helping her with her veil, and buttoning dozens of tiny buttons in the back of a beautiful, white, lacy gown. I imagine being happy for my younger sister on her wedding day.

But it wasn't completely like that; it was a way to escape, the thing she felt she had to do to leave that place before it suffocated her. She

Dana on her wedding day.

Frances on Dana's wedding day. My brother, Mark, quipped that Frances's hat cost more than Dana's wedding dress.

believed she was destined for something more than an old farmhouse outside of Dayton, Ohio.

But there was love once, at least in the beginning. She wrote of how she loved her husband completely and how happy he made her. "*Life is grand!*"

I call this the parallel universe. My biological family was going about its life—like attending a wedding—while I went about mine, completely unaware that the other existed.

Mark said that the morning of Dana's wedding, Dana told Frances that she didn't want to get married. Frances, along with Dana's future mother-in-law, convinced Dana that everything would be fine and that she simply had a case of pre-wedding jitters.

Six months after she was married, Dana had an "accident" while washing glassware and cut her wrist, Mark recalled. She would often spend days in bed. Maybe the jitters she felt the day of her wedding were something more. Maybe she realized that she didn't want to make this man her partner for life. Dana never mentioned a word of any of these struggles in her journals. There was nothing about the trepidation she felt in getting married, nor was there anything written about her ongoing battle with depression. In fact, there were only two entries from the time she was married until July 1985. The struggles that Mark remembered—other than a brief mention of her weight—were completely absent from Dana's journal.

The night before I got married, on July 24, 1982, I sat up alone in the parlor of my parents' house, contemplating whether I should leave because getting married seemed as though it would be a terrible mistake. It was two or three in the morning, and friends who came from out of state were sleeping upstairs. I wanted nothing more than to get in the car and drive away, and the thought of the following day made me physically ill. Could I just leave them all and quietly slip out the door? Where would I go? What would they all think of me? In the end I didn't run away, and the reason was because I didn't want to embarrass my parents.

I began the countdown to my first marriage at the end of my senior year in college.

"*Forty-six days 'til I get married. Me, married. Hard to believe, even for me,*" I wrote the first week of June 1982, not long before I graduated, and when the countdown reached twenty-eight days, I wrote that the thought scared me. I was worried about not only getting married but finding a job. I didn't want to be dependent on a husband. But didn't I seal my own fate by deciding that, a month after graduation, I would get married? While my classmates were meeting with companies and agencies looking for entry-level employees, I was planning a wedding, not actually thinking about a secure future.

At eleven days out, I likened the whole thing to a dream or a bad trip. *"I wish it was over. I wish it never happened. I think that I don't want to get married. I've felt that way for a long time now. Sometimes I wish I could just*

My wedding day, 1982.

run away." I ended that entry with, "*The thought of having kids makes me sick*." And the next day, my journal entry wasn't any better. I wrote that I was scared to get married and I wanted to "*run away from all of it.*"

How did I get to this point? What went wrong?

My first husband and I met at band practice and then saw one another at parties hosted by other musicians. I was auditioning for a group, and that's where we initially talked. One of our mutual friends later told me that after he and I first met, he said, "I'm either going to fuck her or marry her." Like Dana, I was always dreaming of stardom. For me, it was music, especially rock and roll. While she went on and on in her journals about being a famous writer, I was always aspiring to be a famous singer. That I would take up with a musician was completely predictable.

~~◦◦◦~~

When I was a very young child—not much more than five—my kindergarten teacher realized that I had an exceptional voice. "You don't sound like the other children," she told me. I had no idea what she meant. My parents embraced this novelty and made me sing in front of their friends. I was embarrassed, to say the least. I don't think the man who helped my father fix some plumbing in the house cared one bit to hear me sing "America the Beautiful" while he sat on the living room couch flanked by both my parents.

But when I begged them for a piano and lessons, they refused. When I was a freshman in high school, my band director told them that they should find me a private vocal coach in Pittsburgh. Again, they weren't interested, and I was unsuccessful at changing their minds.

Nonetheless, music became my safe space, my therapy, something that was wholly mine. Somewhere in my attic is a small trophy for second place at the school talent show when I was in sixth grade. Two brothers who played "Wipe Out" beat out my rendition of "White Christmas." In high school, my chorus teacher helped me understand scales and theory for regional choir auditions. The sopranos I competed against for chair selection were not only wealthy and beautiful, but they all had private teachers. Still, I was determined and I did okay for someone with absolutely no training. I learned to play guitar well enough to learn some popular songs and began writing my own. I had no qualms about sharing

Me in my dorm room playing my guitar, 1980.

Me in 1984, a band promo shot.

this original music with anyone who would listen. One of my friends in college recorded me singing one of my songs, and not long after, he played it over the speakers at a dance at his fraternity house. I was amazed. I was bitten by the performance bug and there was no turning back.

~~~

By July 1980 we were going out and, for a good long while, I was extremely happy. Unlike so many of my prior relationships, this one started with lots of intense conversations. In late July I wrote, "*I try not to get my hopes up for anything anymore. But I find myself always thinking of the future with him. It sort of scares me.*"

I suppose it was a rock and roll courtship. There was plenty of party-ing, late nights, and a lot of alcohol and drugs. They were always part of the mix. On a trip to Chicago to visit one of his friends, we drove west on I-80 in his Datsun 280Z at 100 mph, listening to Steely Dan and smoking a joint that he rolled while steering the car with his knee.

It wasn't that I didn't love him. I wrote about him constantly in my college journals, from the time we first met until he asked me to marry him. We spent hours and hours talking; we were always going somewhere and doing something. He was funny and smart. But it wasn't enough, this love that we shared. I wasn't near ready—I wasn't even certain that this was what I wanted—and I should have saved us both a whole lot of heartache by calling it off. That one thing would have changed every-thing in my life and his.

On January 24, 1983, I admitted:

> *I've been married for six months. Somehow, lately, I've begun to regret the entire thing. Nothing's the same. He's changed, or maybe I have. It's all falling apart and I don't know why, or maybe I don't care. Something's wrong. I sit and listen, watch, and don't do a thing about anything.*

I wrote of having a constant headache and not deserving to be happy, and the journals that survive from those two years are filled with song lyrics, poems, and chaos.

On January 30, 1984, six months before our marriage ended, I wrote:

> *Reading* Diary of a Mad Housewife *and trying to ignore all the*
> *similarities. Bored. Bored because he is coming home and I'm waiting*
> *here. Waiting. I HATE it. When he was away it was fine. I wasn't*
> *waiting; I was simply living alone.*
> *Yes, I would like to live alone. In my own place, have a job,*
> *and be self sufficient. And I am insecure. Very much so. And I am*
> *unhappy. Very much so . . . trying to make sense out of this marriage.*
> *Hating, with a passion, my monetary dependence.*

Two years to the day after I was married, I left and spent my second anniversary sleeping in my car.

I had no idea what to do or where to go; I had no friends. I rented an unfurnished apartment that contained a borrowed cot and a cooler for food, and I stayed there until I could no longer make rent. My entire life savings was a small inheritance from my aunt. It was a few hundred dollars. It was all I had and I was terrified of having no money and no job. On August 5, I wrote, "It's so strange having nothing."

I called myself a fool and admitted that my whole life was filled with what-ifs and regrets. So many. "*What I'll remember about my youth, if I grow old . . . pain, almosts, what could have been. So far from satisfied. So far from happy.*"

On August 30, 1984, I pondered, "*Where will I be next week, next month? What will I be doing? The excitement of the uncertain. Curiosity. Fascination with the unknown. I will break it down, stretch it to the limit, bend, twist, pry and find the reasons. Then I will go and start over.*"

I left town on a bus in early September that year, red backpack strapped on, thinner than I had ever been, and afflicted with a severe case of acne. I wrote about the strange fascination I had with picking at all the ugly spots on my face. "*Scratch at myself until I bleed. Feel something.*" I headed south to North Carolina to stay with a cousin. It was a disaster. My cousin's marriage wasn't stable, and it didn't take long for his wife to detest my intrusion. I found some part-time work and still dreamed of being a rock star. I envisioned traveling back home in a nice car, wearing a red leather biker jacket and black leather pants. I would show them all, I thought. I can succeed. I auditioned for groups and hoped that something would come my way, but it never did.

"I am having a hard time coping. I'm really uptight about not having a job. I keep thinking bad thoughts. Everything seems dark. I am scared to death of life. I need to work. I need help," I wrote in late September.

While I was in North Carolina, I bought a 1966 Buick Special. I needed a car to even think of finding work. When time dragged on without any hope of a good job, and the situation in my cousin's house became untenable, I drove back to Pennsylvania.

It was the only time I ever borrowed money from my adoptive parents. And they made sure I repaid every penny.

My adoptive parents grew up poor, so money was extremely important to them and paying back debts was non-negotiable. What I didn't know was their biological son had been stealing them blind for years. He began pilfering money from them as early as college, and by the time he was in his mid-thirties, he had burned through their entire life savings.

I was nearly five when my adoptive mother gave birth to him, and I still remember the day he was born. It was late July and I was with a friend of the family, waiting outside on a bench on the hospital grounds. I wasn't allowed in to visit her—it was adults only at that time—but I recall waving to her through her hospital window. She was in her mid-forties by then, and I recollect snippets of the conversation among family members. It was a miracle, they said. A blessing. Finally, they would have a child of their own. When he was younger, I stood up for him when other kids picked on him, but we were never, ever close. It was as though he and I existed in separate worlds.

They loved him with a fierce passion, and for years they told me that I should be successful like him, that I should find a job that made a lot of money like him. I was the disappointment. I really no longer mattered.

⁓◦⊙◦⁓

A month after she was married, Dana dreamed of having children. She thought if she had a boy, she would name him Dominic—Nikki for short. If a girl, she would be Rosa. *"Right now is one of the happiest times of my life,"* she said. That contentment was brief, and despite always wanting to escape her home, she found herself missing it after her husband accepted a job in North Carolina. "She was bitter about the move because it moved her away from Mom," Mark explained. "She had no one in North Carolina. She didn't make friends easily." Dana wrote: "*I can't believe that I miss my home. My room with its sagging, discolored paper and hot as hell. So many summer nights staring out that screen watching and hearing the world go by me.*"

I knew that room. Nearly every time I visited Frances in Dayton, I slept in Dana's room. It was tiny, with a sloped ceiling and a cubby hole for storage. It had one window that looked over the farm fields that stretched out in every direction. There was a grape arbor, a huge garden, outbuildings, and ancient trees. Sometimes, during these visits, my relationship with Frances seemed refreshingly normal, as though I had always been a part of her life. We grilled in the backyard, played cards, shopped together, and looked at old photos. One year, when she had a bumper crop of green peppers, she mailed me a huge box of them so I could can pepper relish.

I slept in that room one summer, and it *was* hot as hell. But it was quaint and a place where a young girl could read and dream and hope for the future.

As Dana's life became more chaotic, she leaned on the journals more and more. But in the early years of her marriage, there were big gaps in entries, sometimes months at a time. What was written reflected a woman who was unsettled and moving far from the halcyon days of a newlywed. She wrote of feeling suffocated, of sleeping her life away. Her dreams dissolved into the dull routine of marriage, and boredom ruled her days. She knew she should get a job but wrote, "*I just can't force myself. I don't know why.*"

And the issues she had with her weight became front and center in almost all of her journal entries.

On June 20, 1986, she was still very much in love with her husband, confessing that she found "*such sweet oblivion*" being in his arms. But she was frustrated with her body. She weighed 209 pounds. "*Dear God! Such obesity!*" she wrote. She was looking forward to a trip from North Carolina back to Dayton, and she hoped she would have lost enough weight to "*earn new pants. Fashionable. Tops and jeans and new shoes.*"

In August 1986, three years into her marriage, she conceded, *"Life is so different from what I thought it would be."* She still dreamed of visiting Scotland and England and how her life *"could have been."* Again, she toyed with the idea of having a child, *"something that's mine."* She dismissed the thought by December when her biggest worry was that *"no one will ever know I'm here."*

The desire to be remembered. The desire to be worshipped. The desire for material possessions. All three would become front and center in her life.

Dana at Christmas, undated photo.

CHAPTER 7

A WAGON FULL OF HEARTACHE

At twenty-four, Dana often felt that her life was over, and she referred to her marriage as a wagon full of heartache. Two months before I turned twenty-four, I left my first husband after two years of marriage.

In early April 1987, Dana wrote that she wanted to be beautiful by her twenty-fourth birthday. She wanted piano lessons, a horse, a computer, a house, and nice furniture, and she expected her husband to provide these things. But she knew that most of it was out of reach—Dana's tastes were far more extravagant than what they could afford as a young couple—and it frustrated her.

"*I can't stand him lately,*" she said of her husband two months before she turned twenty-four. "*I think I'll get thin and divorce him.*" She didn't get thin. Not then. She didn't divorce him. Not then. But she did decide to enroll in college so she could be "*cultured and educated.*"

In August 1987, Dana felt that college would help her make her life come together.

"*Hello, I've gone and done it. College. Me . . . Yes college. I feel good about that,*" she wrote, weaving in comments about not only taking the significant step of furthering her education but also about losing weight and reaching a goal of 108 pounds. "*I want to start new on my birthday. Next year I'll be slim and gorgeous! Oooh. Concentrate on diet and studies,*" she wrote a week before she turned twenty-four.

"*These things give me hope. So much I want a second chance to make something of my life,*" she penned on August 25. She was upbeat and contemplated auditioning for a musical or maybe the college choir. However, a week later her journal entry centered around how school was a disappointment, complaining that the girls are "*hateful*."

"*Why doesn't anyone see it?*" she lamented on September 3. "*I can't have it. I can never have it. I can't go through chorus again. I'm too old for it. Maybe it's my weight. Anyway, I'm not quite as powerful as before. Mediocrity. It's my middle name. Can't see past the tears.*"

She was auditioning for a part in a college production and was preparing herself for the disappointment of not being chosen. She must have gotten the part, though, because a few days later she wrote, "*The picture is a bit brighter now. Hoping someday to be a star. I am feeling powerful again.*" There were a few entries about the production but not much detail. Only that it went well.

Interestingly, the *Pensacola News Journal* published a photo of Dana and her two castmates in a production of *The Miss Firecracker Contest*. Not only that, she was nominated for an award for that performance. None of this ever made it into the pages of her journal.

Comments on school, however, became a passing thing. Dana's growing obsession was Jim Brown. She devoted most of her writing from mid-August 1987 and through most of 1988 to him. Jim Brown was the boy whom she first wrote about in her journal when she was a teenager. Mark explained that Dana, Frank, and Jim all attended the same church, and that's where she met both boys. They had a long history together, Mark added, and Dana was enticed by Jim's recklessness and his frequent brushes with the law.

"*Jim. I can't beat this thing. He still crowds my thoughts. He must hear me—must tell me how it is with him . . . Does he still dream of me? Remember those days of our closeness? Those few touches we shared,*" she wrote in the first entry of a new journal on August 10.

She called him many, many times and, in her mind, created a full-blown relationship with him in her journals. She was absolutely obsessive about him, and she relished the fact that her husband was blind to what she was doing. "*Oooh my power! Dana, the bitch!*"

Jim wasn't a particularly handsome man, but he was just dangerous enough for Dana to be addictively attracted to him. He was in trouble with the law more than once and that had a certain appeal to her. She loved the thrill of this lifestyle and she wanted to be part of it.

"Perhaps he's toying with me. Maybe not. I wish I could see him again. I would love to know how I would be with him. I am concentrating on becoming beautiful. Then when I would see him he could not resist me. Would I? What would stop me?"

Even then she believed she would not always be with Frank. *"Someday,"* she wrote, *"I will move on to greater things. I believe I can. Viciously I will use."*

Every entry in her journal was at least in part centered around Jim, and on October 17 she revealed, *"Spoke with Jim. He pledged his love."* In an entry in mid-December 1987, she wondered whether she really wanted to be with Jim or just enjoyed the drama.

"What the hell am I destroying myself for? I'm afraid for myself. The ass said he'd be home and he's not, so I wait like a nervous flighty 12 year old. I can't give up my prosperity. Yes, I'm a bitch. I can't believe myself. I'm playing too close to the edge. I'm afraid I'll fall off."

Despite this rant, she wrote that her heart and head ached for him and how incredible he was at expressing his love to her.

At the beginning of February 1988, Dana began a daily countdown of days and hours when she was to finally meet Jim at the end of the month. She wrote him letters in her journal, wondering whether she had the strength to leave her husband for this man whom she hadn't seen in years.

"I'm bleeding, weeping, broken and I'm terrified. I'm crying in darkness—deep darkness. Can you find me? Can I find my way out? Will you give to me what I need . . . I'm drowning and you shall either save me or push me to my death," she wrote on February 25.

She eventually left Frank for Jim and indulged herself in a short-lived affair with him.

On March 10, 1988, Dana questioned her actions. *"What is his appeal? I can't grasp it. It's not physical, but it is . . . He does not cherish me. I need that. Perhaps I am attracted because I cannot sway him."*

Jim had an ex and a child, and Dana was jealous of both. After a month of being with him, he stopped touching her, but that was okay with Dana because it was part of the game. She couldn't tolerate a man she could manipulate.

On March 20, she wrote, *"Except for last night's talk this weekend has been shit. Sometimes I'm so unsure, but it's part of the allure of it all."* A day later she asked herself why she was with him. And at the end of March, she contemplated leaving Jim but didn't know where she would go. "*I speak with Frank and wonder. Happiness? Where is it? Jim or Frank?*" And on the following page of her journal, she added, "*He's [Jim's] a liar and I can't believe he treats me the way he does.*"

She admitted to be "*destructively drawn to his treatment of me.*" In one entry she described Jim as "*beautifully unstable, yet so incredibly dangerous.*"

By July the affair was over, and Dana—still separated from her husband—again talked about going back to school. Instead she hooked up with a heavy metal band called Sacred Rite. As with many life changes that I would have considered important enough to write about, Dana didn't offer much detail about the months she spent with this group. She could have been their manager or merchandise seller, but she never quite spelled it out. Mark said he has absolutely no recollection of where she met these musicians and how she ended up traveling with them. The only thing he remembers is that she gave him a band T-shirt.

She wrote about the partying they all did and some of the cities she traveled to for gigs. That, too, was short-lived.

All the while she was still looking for this mysterious man who she felt was her destiny, one who would "*rock my world.*"

By September she felt that she was in control of herself and believed she could be happy with Frank. She wrote that she felt better and that while she felt sorry for Jim, it was over between them. "*The stupidity of past months is painful to read.*"

By November 1988, she was home again. Frank took her back.

When I asked Mark why Frank would have Dana back in his life after all she had done, he said it was simple: he loved her.

In December 1988, not long before Christmas and at nearly twenty-five-and-a-half years old, Dana found out she was pregnant. She never wrote anything about the reason why, whether it was planned or her way of trying to mend her marriage, but she did write extensively about this huge change in her life.

She couldn't decide what to feel or how to process those feelings. She felt maternal. She felt lonely. She mourned the loss of her freedom. And yet, she believed the relationship with her husband was "*wonderful*" because of the pregnancy.

"*Who would have believed it possible,*" she wrote. "*Certainly not me.*"

Frances traveled to Florida for the birth and Dana felt "*suffocated beyond belief*" by her presence. Frances may have been an overbearing mother figure, but she gave Dana what she didn't have with the birth of her first two children: someone who cared and loved her.

Less than a week before her eldest daughter was born, Dana disclosed this:

> *I know what I know—there's a level to life little felt or understood.*
> *I can see glimpses of it in myself and sometimes others. It helps me to*
> *understand and channel my power. Very few share my thoughts on*
> *this. I don't have it with Frank. But I don't think I'm supposed to. I*
> *am little of this world.*

It was the first written glimpse of Dana's belief that she held a sixth sense.

Mark said Dana had always thought she held some sort of supernatural power. He remembered her dabbling in the occult when she was a teenager. When something bad happened to someone she didn't particularly like, Dana believed that it was the result of a spell she had cast and that their misfortune was her doing.

Dana gave birth on August 17, 1989, and she vowed that her daughter "*will have the opportunities and care*" that her life lacked. "*I have regrets and fears about the death of my freedom . . . but hopes for the future. I can pen my way there,*" she added in this entry, dated September 6, 1989.

She called motherhood "*strange, frightening and exhilarating*" and realized, in hearing her daughter cry, "*just how much responsibility I have.*" She also promised to write her a letter for the future, and she seemed to have a sense of peace. Still, being a new mother didn't keep Dana from complaining of being bored out of "*my fucking mind*" and needing space of her own.

The desire for fame resurfaced and she believed the journals were her key to greatness.

She began a new journal on September 7, 1989. This small, cloth-bound book was covered in flowers that were shades of browns, tans, and teal blues. The background was a deep red. In her initial entries, she wrote of her *"undying compulsion to write and record my life."* As she often did, she addressed the journal directly: *"Many years from now you will be part of my legacy . . . as for now, you are my comfort."*

It had also been a year since she had been with the Sacred Rite band, and she missed that life, *"the drugs and alcohol and the 'riot' atmosphere. I can't have it again and I probably shouldn't anyway,"* she admitted.

At the same time Dana was learning to navigate the role of new mom, she developed an obsession for Led Zeppelin singer Robert Plant. Mark said he had no clue as to why, but it may have been that she and Jim listened to Zeppelin together and she felt some sort of connection to him through the music. Nonetheless, Zeppelin was one of her favorite bands and "The Rain Song" was on repeat in her house. She called the band her opium, *"calming, exhilarating and sensual. It is an integral part of my psyche. It helps me feel."*

While this fantasy seemed to give her a mental break from her new reality of motherhood, the lines blurred between what was going on in her head and what was happening in her life. She admitted her obsession with the musician *"sometimes distorts my reality,"* and she insisted that she must meet him. At the same time, she worried that he would die before she became famous.

Mark said that Dana actually did get the chance to meet Plant after a concert. He saw her, said hello, and moved on. This meeting couldn't have been more unremarkable or any less magical. Dana would often associate dreams and coincidence with destiny, he added. This made her feel as though she had a mental connection with someone. Robert Plant was the perfect example.

With her first child only a month old, Dana wrote, *"I am firm in my decision to have no other children. I don't think it selfish, I think it wise. I must have the freedom to work and travel as I need."* Dana was developing a screenplay, and she hoped that *"someday it will be the way to my dreams,"* but there were never entries in the journals celebrating something finished.

Mark said that she did finish it and sent it out to publishers. It was rejected and, as far as he knows, she never submitted another manuscript. Dana didn't handle criticism well, Mark told me. Rather than revise her work based on comments from prospective publishers, she simply abandoned that particular project and sank into depression.

She tried to balance writing with caring for her daughter, and she was often frustrated that she didn't have enough time to work on her craft. Moreover, her journal entries were obsessively centered around losing weight, and near the holidays—a year after she had last seen him—she often wrote about Jim and how she still missed him. *"If we only lived forever . . . I love you still, Jim. Maybe somehow we can both comfort in that. Perhaps another lifetime."*

These occasional entries aside, Dana seemed happy with her life. She said Frank was a good father *"and I could not survive this without him . . . as of now things are stable enough and I pray they stay that way."* But as always seemed to be the case in Dana's life, any sense of peace was short-lived.

CHAPTER 8

SETTING THE STAGE FOR CHANGE

Dana hid her struggles well. To everyone around her, she seemed sure of herself, confident. To her brother, Mark, she was a fun-loving, witty, and devoted sister. But what she shared with her journal was much less optimistic.

The year 1990 brought more disappointment. Dana was bored and restless and yearned for a change in her life. At least that's what she wrote in her journal. Mark, though, remembered things differently. This Dana wasn't necessarily the person that Mark knew.

Dana was so much fun to be around, he remembered. He spent summers with her after she was married and they were extremely close. There were many entries in her journals devoted to how much she adored her younger brother.

"I love my brother so much now. He's quite a person."

"I love him terribly and our relationship has never been closer."

"Mark gone. Miss him most of all. I love seeing him so much. I wish he would have stayed."

Mark said that during this time in her life, Dana was not only a positive influence, but she gave him the means to leave an unstable home life.

Mark told me that arguments were a regular occurrence at home between Frances and Frank, Mark's dad. Sometimes, these fights would last for days. Frances knew how to push Frank's buttons and she could be absolutely relentless. On the other hand, Mark's father was an extremely jealous man.

Mark told me that for the longest time, his father wouldn't allow Frances to get a driver's license. When she had her ears pierced, he was convinced she was having an affair, and when she finally learned to drive and got a job, he accused her of seeing other men.

Dana was living in Florida when Mark was a senior in high school, and she demanded that he be allowed to stay with her after graduation and attend college there. She gave him the opportunity to escape, and so he did. It changed his life.

In early 1990, when her eldest daughter was about seven months old, Dana began keeping track of her cycle because she didn't want any more children. But she added this caveat: "*Not Frank's.*" These words came as a surprise since earlier in the month, she wrote, "*Sometimes I find myself truly needing and loving Frank.*" Perhaps she hoped that her mysterious, promised man would be the father of any future children.

She continued to work on a screen play and by mid-April she wrote that she was editing it. On April 19 she said that the editing was complete. With it done, she talked about writing another.

Her weight was front and center again. She weighed 165 pounds and complained about how gross she looked in a swimsuit. On April 30, she wrote, "*The baby screams and I hide myself away and wish for better. My weight is fucking out of control.*"

An entry on June 7 was the first time she mentioned reading tarot cards. She believed that her ability to "*discern the supernatural has increased drastically,*" and she got very serious about learning the tarot.

"*It feels right, as if I had done it before and the cards are alive,*" she penned on June 9, 1990.

Internally she was struggling with motherhood. She was struggling to feel.

In early September, Dana's wish was this: "*I long for anything—even tragedy to change the state of my life.*" Later that month she was pregnant again. "*I don't know what any of it means . . . I feel tossed aimlessly through my life.*" Having another child was the last thing she wanted.

Dana offered very little during her second pregnancy. She insisted that her life was so boring she hadn't needed to make an entry. "*My heart is empty. I am lonely and alone,*" she wrote on December 6.

Surprisingly, she also wrote very little about the birth of her second child in May 1991, even though it nearly killed her. There was only one mention of it.

In a brief entry she wrote, "*I won't do that again.*"

According to Mark, Dana died during the delivery of her youngest daughter and had to be resuscitated. Whatever her near-death experience, it brought about a significant transformation. "She said she had a horrifying experience," he told me. "Hellish. Dark. She started to change at that point. She wouldn't talk about it at all."

Distressing near-death experiences have been well documented, but few people who endure the terror of this type of event will share what happened. Mark said he saw a marked change in Dana afterward. It was as though she felt that if this was all there was to life, she didn't want to spend what remaining time she had stuck in a marriage with two children.

She wrote that she missed her body, her sexuality, the person she used to be. She had managed to reach 155 pounds for her birthday in 1990, but after the birth of her youngest daughter in May, she once again weighed nearly 200 pounds. Mark said she would rarely leave the house or even get dressed. Her life was far from what she wanted. Mark and his wife often wondered whether Dana suffered from postpartum depression.

On July 28, 1991, she bemoaned, "*My birthday comes soon. 28. Inside I feel 10 years younger. If it could all be done again . . . God, I could have been anything.*"

A day before her twenty-eighth birthday, she wrote, "*Please death, take me in my sleep.*" Other than that wish, nearly every entry focused on her struggle to lose weight and she wondered, "*Why can't I stop putting food in my mouth?*" She needed to convince herself that she was a "*naturally thin person*" and that she made eating choices like a thin person. "*I am thin and lovely and worthy,*" and if she could just manage to lose another twenty pounds, everything would be better.

Dana and I shared an obsession with weight, and, though I didn't write about it anywhere nearly as much as she did, the desire to be thin was a huge part of my life. I first became aware of how I looked when I was about eleven years old. Our class was waiting outside the school for the bus to arrive that would take us on our sixth-grade class trip to Niagara Falls, and I recall looking at what I was wearing and then scanning the outfits of my classmates. Even at that age I envied the girls in my class who were thin. I stared at my bulging stomach in ill-fitting pants and I despised how I looked. Everything about me was wrong. That following summer, between sixth and seventh grade, I decided I was going to get thin, and I did. I rode my bicycle hundreds of miles, I swam, I played ball, I ate a whole lot less, and I dropped a significant amount of weight. It would be the first of many times.

I was away the summer before my senior year in high school, and when I got back home my boyfriend told me that I had gotten fat. It's strange how well I remember that moment. I was sitting on the couch in his parents' house, and I was wearing a pair of bib overalls and a tank top. Our relationship was ending, and it was a cruel dig at how I looked, something said in anger to hurt me.

Again, I took control. I became a distance runner. I began a serious journey into cooking but never eating. I became anorexic at a time when not much was said about the disorder. It wasn't a new disease by any stretch, but in the 1970s, in rural Pennsylvania, it wasn't something anyone talked about. At least not anyone that I knew.

In my high school journal, in a section called "Dialogue with the Body," I wrote often about struggling with my weight during my junior and senior year. I chided myself for being out of shape and fat, but by May 1978, I was thrilled that I weighed eighty-eight pounds. I wrote that I wanted to lose three more, "just for the hell of it," and I did.

I weighed eighty-three pounds when I graduated from high school. In my freshman year of college, I weighed seventy-two pounds. Like my sister, I too have had lifelong issues with self-image. The quote, "no woman can be too rich or too thin" stuck with me for years, and there was never a time in my life when I felt I was ever thin enough.

CHAPTER 9

HARBINGER

There wasn't a gradual transition into Wicca, at least in the journals. While Mark talked about Dana dabbling with spells when she was a teen, she never wrote about it. But beginning in the first months of 1992, Dana was learning to cast spells to fulfill her desires.

By early 1992, Dana began her journey into the pagan movement Wicca, or perhaps it was then that she actually made a concerted effort to embrace the path she always felt she traveled. Dana was drawn to the Norse religion, and it wasn't long before pages of her journals contained notes on the tarot, tarot readings, and Runes.

In January, Dana wrote that she was refining her rituals and "*casting to relieve my agony of the past.*" As was the case with many of her entries, the agony that she wanted to banish remained unmentioned. She believed she was becoming psychic. She sought beauty and money and assistance for her family. In February, she declared, "*I need to read the tarot for profit. Practice magic for my better welfare. I need books. I need time to be. To become. Slow and steady wins the race. I'm so alone. So separated. So desperate.*"

Much of this desperation seemed to be directly related to her failed attempt to lose any significant amount of weight. Not long after she lost five pounds, she gained seven. The goal to become thin consumed page after page of her journal.

And yet, in the early months of 1992, Dana was more optimistic than she had been in a very long time. On February 22, she noted, "*I have two* daughters. *They are lovely and interesting and they will challenge the world. I have a husband of nearly nine years and an extremely comfortable existence. I also have a budding career. My story ideas swirl in my mind.*" But Dana—at least in the pages of her journal—could never embrace any long-term contentment. Nearly a week later she wrote that she felt trapped—so trapped she *"could die."*

"I lay here on the floor swamped and prodded by children and an existence I despise. If for a night I could be distracted by a man who would be interested in just me. I'm not gonna make it today. Nope. I'm gone. Fuck the universe."

By early May 1992, Dana was keeping two journals. One recorded day-to-day life and the other focused on Wicca. She titled it her "Book of Mirrors," and in it she talked about spells and her desire to school herself in the craft.

"I feel as if my spiritual quest has ended and can be fulfilled by Wicca," she wrote on May 3, 1992. *"My first casting of the circle was sloppy, but sincere. My candle burning spell, I believe, was particularly effective. Runes, candles, and colors draw my interest the most. I feel the need to gather my tools and commence. I feel the need to know and be known by the Goddess and God."*

It was something she always felt was a part of her, ever since she was an adolescent. She believed she had some sort of power, that she was different, not of this world. She sincerely believed that she was chosen in some way. *"I intend on being a witch and am thrilled by this,"* she wrote when her youngest daughter was nearly a year old. She felt as though she found a home with this path.

On June 1, she penned:

I feel myself stirring. I feel the control. I feel the anticipation of powerful magic . . . I never knew how badly I wanted Wicca until it was taken from me. I can bring much to the gods. I am different. I am knowing of much. I have a wisdom and an even judgement . . . I have a burning—greater for this than anything I have ever felt . . .

In the summer of 1992, Dana and her husband opened a restaurant. It was called "Franco's, Pensacola's Great Little Italian Restaurant." Frances helped with the venture. She was an excellent cook and had worked in the food industry for years. She knew her way around a commercial kitchen, she understood menus, and she understood customers. Mark told me that when Frances was involved with its management, food preparation, and recipe development, the restaurant was wildly successful. Its tasty home-made Italian dishes and atmosphere were a draw for many retirees who were of Italian descent. Frances would routinely take time to talk to the customers, and this rapport not only kept them coming back but helped grow the business. Frances was everything that Dana wasn't.

Dana alienated the customers, according to Mark. He explained that once Frances stopped being involved with the restaurant, beer seemed to be selling better than food, so they closed the restaurant and opened a bar in another part of town.

"You can't screw up, 'Here's a beer,'" Mark said.

I always found it strange that Dana left out most of the details of this part of her life. She complained about being bored, but it would be diffi-cult to find the time to even take a breath when operating a restaurant and caring for two small children. What she seemed to want more than any-thing was someone to desire her. She felt lonely, desperate, and unloved. She craved attention. She looked for it in the patrons of the bar, and she became particularly interested in a man who rode a Harley. Much to her surprise, he refused to take the bait. She complained that he was a biker with a conscience, with morals, and she gave up trying to seduce him.

In 1993, Dana escaped again. She left her husband. Her children. Her life.

Dana vanished from the pages of her journals, and Polgara was born. *"I am a witch. I am a magician. I am knowing. I am Polgara,"* Dana wrote in late January 1993.

Polgara was a sorceress in a fictional tale, a fantasy saga written by David Eddings. Dana first took this name in late May 1992 to transition from who she was—a wife and a mother of two who considered her life boring and mundane—to someone extraordinary.

Polgara would be a maker of spells and a reader of cards. She would take Dana's place.

Dana was forever reinventing herself and Polgara was the latest iteration.

CHAPTER 10

MY ORPHAN SOUL

On November 17, 1984, I wrote, "My life is ridiculous. Totally. I believe I'll end it soon. Quietly." I had contemplated suicide times before and times after. Sometimes I felt completely disconnected from anyone and anything. I felt as though I was trapped inside a glass booth, able to see but not touch or communicate. Sylvia Plath's The Bell Jar comes to mind. The book spoke to me at nineteen, and I obsessed over it in my college English journal, so much so that one of my professors took me aside and encouraged me to talk to her if I needed to. I felt as though I was descending into that same sort of madness in the late autumn of 1984, and all that was happening in my life was a painful reminder of college. I wonder, at times, whether I ever moved beyond those days.

In the years that Dana's marriage was unraveling, I was trying to piece my life together. When I returned to Pennsylvania in late 1984, I had no job and was forced to live with my parents. The reasons I left my first husband were many, but one certainly was because I'd fallen in love with someone else. On Christmas Eve, 1984, I wrote, "*The past haunts me, the future scares me, and the present is like a battle zone.*"

In early 1985, my partner, Mark, and I moved in together, and in 1986, the year our daughter was born, I was working as a waitress. I was happy to have some sort of income but certainly not happy with the situation. Much of the clientele at the diner where I worked were truckers, and I took a lot of ribbing during my pregnancy. But most of them were extremely kind and thought of me as a daughter. They were much kinder than my employers.

Two days before I gave birth, Mark was admitted to the hospital with a back injury. He was on one floor and I was on another. I was told he couldn't be there for our child's birth because of hospital rules. I've always wondered if it was because we weren't married at the time. Ironically, my birth experience was much like my mother's. I was alone, with only the nursing staff to coach me through labor and delivery.

After my six weeks of maternity leave were over, my employers informed me they didn't need my services full time, that someone else had taken my position at the restaurant. With Mark on leave from his job until his back was healed and me without any full-time employment, I was forced to apply for food stamps. I was embarrassed to use them, keenly aware of the stigma of a single mother taking advantage of the welfare system rather than working. Unlike Dana, who was constantly searching for a man to take care of her, I harbored a profound fear of not having a job and money, and of losing what little I did have.

My first break came a year later, when I found a part-time job as a freelance reporter for a local newspaper. That part-time gig eventually turned into a full-time job in late 1988.

It was a much-needed and much-welcome change. We eventually moved to Ridgway, where *The Ridgway Record* was located, bought a house, and married in 1989. I dove headfirst into this new career and loved the connection I felt to the community I served and the many ways the newspaper staff could give it a voice.

~~⋘⋙~~

My daughter grew up with a mother who was the "newspaper lady." When she was older she would come with me to the office on Friday night when it was my turn to put out Saturday's paper. She sat in the lunchroom with her Walkman and sketch pad while I worked. When I look back, I realize I worked so much—I wanted more than anything to be successful and recognized as a good journalist—that I missed a substantial chunk of her childhood. I made sure she had the piano lessons I was denied when a child, but I was often so tired at the end of the day that I would be too exhausted to help her with her piano lessons and homework. Now in her mid-thirties, my daughter insists that I was a wonderful mother. I don't see it that way.

It was during these first few years at the paper that a fellow staffer wrote an article about a birth mother searching for the child she gave up for adoption decades earlier. I recall feeling bad for this woman, and I thought of my own birth mother. I wondered whether she remembered me and what the circumstances were around my birth. It may have been the first time in a decade that I gave any serious thought to the woman who gave birth to me. It was enough to encourage me to finally begin my own search.

Between 1993 and 1996, I amassed a huge amount of search and support material. There were newsletters from the Pittsburgh Adoption Connection and other adoption support groups, tips on searching, and names and phone numbers of other adoptees and birth mothers in the northwest region of Pennsylvania. The internet was in its infancy then, and there was no local provider, so any time spent online was charged by the minute, like a long-distance call. There was no social media, no Ancestry, no 23AndMe. There was just old-fashioned sleuthing and a lot of luck.

I became the go-to reporter at the newspaper for birth mothers and adoptees who were searching for birth families that had some type of link to Elk County, Pennsylvania. I also reported on legislation moving through the Pennsylvania House and Senate on adoption law.

The year 1993 also saw the formation of a local adoption support group organized by an adoptee from nearby St. Marys. The group met monthly, and members did what they could to assist others with their searches. One by one, many of the group located either birth mothers or children given up for adoption. Everyone who connected with a member of their birth family had powerful stories to share, and not all of them were good. In one instance, a birth mother who had been raped in college told her daughter that she would meet her once to give her family history and medical information but wanted no further contact. Another member, a birth mother who was a tremendous and loving person and forced to give away her baby by her parents, was thrilled when she located her son. He, though, was angry that she had abandoned him and wanted nothing to do with her. Another adoptee found a huge extended family who couldn't have been happier that he was now part of the clan.

In 1994, a birth mother from DuBois, Pennsylvania, put an ad in the *Record* entitled "LOST DAUGHTER."

> *Happy Birthday to a blond-haired, blue-eyed 7 lbs. 12 oz. Beautiful baby girl. You were born on July 4th, 1962, 11:59 P.M. at the Salvation Army Unwed Mother's Home in Pittsburgh, Pa. During that period, I a 16 year-old unwed mother was sent away and returned home without my baby against my wishes. A part of me will never be whole until I learn of your whereabouts.*

I eventually wrote a feature on her, and it gave me insight as to what it was like for a young woman in the early 1960s, who was pregnant and unmarried. She was forced to quit high school, her parents sent her away, and she was unable to keep her child. Each year she said she celebrated her daughter's birthday alone. "That's my day. I feel I messed up, and I pay for that day every year . . ."

I had been searching for a year when I wrote that feature, and I hoped that my birth mother still thought of me in the same way as the birth mom from DuBois.

When I was relinquished as a newborn, the agency that handled my adoption, Catholic Charities, was the keeper of what facts existed about my life. I was only *allowed* to see what was termed "non-identifying" information—the stuff that told you the nationality of your birth mom (and birth father, if known) as well as their ages, height, weight, eye color, hair color, any siblings, parents, intelligence level, and so on. To even get this far, my request had to be in the form of a notarized letter to the agency.

The letter that contained my non-identifying information was typed on Catholic Charities's letterhead and dated March 22, 1993. I was afraid to open it. I was nearly thirty-three, and until that letter arrived in the mail, I knew absolutely nothing about my biological family history. I stared at the two pages of background information for a very long time, and I read it over and over. It was the closest I had come to knowing who I was.

The hitch was this: My birth mother wasn't from Pennsylvania, and the agency considered my birth mother's state of residence "identifying" information. It was as though if I knew what state she lived in prior to traveling to Erie, I would somehow immediately find her. Catholic Charities wasn't able to locate her, and the caseworker said she wasn't allowed to tell me my birth mother's state of residence.

I wrote to the Erie County Court, hoping to obtain additional information, and in a letter dated June 30, 1993, the Orphan's Court investigator indicated she couldn't find anything more on either of my birth parents. She closed by noting she would retain my letter in her files "in the event that your natural parents ever attempt to contact you through this office." She, too, was unable to tell me where my mother resided.

It took an attorney to petition the court to have that one piece of information released.

In a letter from the Erie County judge, dated July 27, 1995, I finally learned where my birth mother lived before she was sent away. She was from New York.

In three years of searching, one thing remained with me. When I discovered that my birth mother was from New York, I placed ads in papers located in western New York, not far from Erie. Although I didn't locate my mother through these ads, I did hear from a number of women who had relinquished their babies in 1960. They hoped that I might be their daughter. Some told me their stories. It was heartbreaking.

As I was navigating courts, Catholic Charities, dead ends, and frustration, Dana was transforming her life again.

While I was searching for a family, she was throwing hers away.

CHAPTER 11

PRETTY POLLY

In the American murder ballad "Pretty Polly," a young woman is seduced by her lover and falls prey to his wicked ways. When I first discovered that Dana had changed her name to Polly, it wasn't Polgara the Sorceress that came to mind, but poor Pretty Polly, stabbed to death by her man.

Dana—now calling herself Polgara, or Polly, for short—traveled to New Orleans in early August 1993 for a vacation. "*I will have New Orleans for my birthday—and the full moon!! Who can say what will happen for me,*" she wrote on July 22, 1993.

In a prophetic entry two days later, she said, "*Do I really desire to leave here and give up my life and my money as it shall come? My kids? The familiarity of him and union that's 12 years old . . . but no matter what, I shall have the full moon and my birthday in that extraordinary place.*" The trip was a crossroads for Dana, and she believed that when she returned, she wouldn't be the same person. There had also been cracks in her relationship with her brother, Mark. She called him "*sad, blind and not really a part of me. What a shame, to have grown beyond even that. Oh well.*" There was no reason given for why she felt this way, but it was the beginning of a shift. Dana and Frances were often at odds, but Mark, her little brother, had always been a huge part of her life. This relationship, too, was changing.

The day following *Lughnasadh*, the first of the harvest festivals on August 1, Dana arrived in New Orleans and wasted no time creating a new life for herself despite this supposedly being a vacation.

On August 3, she penned, "*The stones from the street cry out to me. The walls of the buildings beckon me. There are those that live here and love here. I want to be one of them.*" Not only that, she insisted she didn't miss her children or her husband.

She didn't want to go back home. Dana wrote that her children could survive without her, that perhaps they could live with their grandparents. She could visit them monthly. That would work. She wanted out. "*I am sorry, I can't go back. I can't go back. I can't look at him. I can't sleep with him. I have a right to be happy.*"

I don't believe she ever intended to go back to her marriage even before she left for New Orleans. While she wrote about looking forward to walking cobblestone streets, seeing the cathedral, and visiting the magic shops, there was also a man waiting for her there. She called him Fritz, her "warrior." She never wrote about when and where she met him. He simply appeared on the page earlier that summer, another lover, it seemed. He showed up in many journal entries not long after she arrived in New Orleans. But his origins are never divulged in the pages. It seems he may have been an artist, but Dana's words were as much a mystery as some of the people in her life.

"*He sleeps without moving and he snores. Were he to have someone to care for, he would take better care of himself. I cannot tell you what will be. I saw that he loved me three weeks ago. He is so simple, yet so complex. He is so single-minded, yet so diverse,*" Dana described Fritz. She said that she could not make him love her. She could only wait for him to choose whether he wanted her in his life.

At 7:53 P.M. on August 3, she offered this: "*This is probably my last entry of this day. I shall be extremely beautiful this evening and perhaps some-one will want me. Who can say what will befall me . . . whether he will take me or cast me away. I am weary now. I pray my sleep brings me, first, dreams of prophecy and, secondly, peace. I love you F.*" After this she wrote, "*Love and light, and all that's right, hear my might, make me irresistible tonight!*"

The next day she told the journal that she was pleased with how the evening turned out. She felt beautiful and wrote that three men—at least—wanted her affection and attention. Dana desired everything she'd read and dreamed about as a teenager. She craved romance, mys-tery, caresses, lust. She looked for it over and over, with Jim Brown and other affairs. The old and magical city of New Orleans seemed to be the perfect place for these dreams to come to fruition. She was absolutely captivated.

Early on August 4, she waited for the light so that she could take her journal and pen, eat a croissant, write, and *"dream of what it would be like to be here every day of my life."*

She described later that morning the flurry of traffic at a cafe near the market:

> *A man is sweetly kissing the keys of a piano near by and the blues of the world seeps from his throat. I have nothing left but a peach, my money spent on a cheese croissant and orange juice. I desire to meet someone to immortalize in my book today. I feel so light today. I have felt this since Sunday. One moment—the music enchants me.*

In these first days in New Orleans, Dana described her surroundings with beautiful detail: *"Music just erupted from a riverboat docked close to me and a trolley skidded by and someone's wash is hanging to dry in the tree I sit beneath. I have this insatiable urge to carve my name and his in this bench. And now a train blasts by. We are now immortalized in wood."*

Dana was jolted back to reality when she talked to Frank, her husband of a dozen years, who wanted to heal their relationship. At this point, all she wanted was a way out.

She pushed it all aside to continue to dream of having her own apartment, her own life, and a chance at happiness. *"I could write and write and write! I could live and breathe and be well inside."*

She had made up her mind. This vacation wasn't a vacation at all, but the first step in ending one life and beginning another. *"I shall be here by November. Fritz and I shall be who we are."* Later that night—August 4—she said her call to Frank weighed her down immeasurably. But then she thought of Fritz and his voice and how he made her feel. *"I smiled and that bit of a rush I feel is so wonderful."* She believed she deserved happiness, and despite feeling sad for her husband and children, and being torn about it all, she seemed intent on staying. Staying with Fritz, her lover *"who is not yet my lover."*

On the evening of August 10, Dana wrote that she was disheartened she couldn't truly be what her husband wanted or needed. She insisted she wished only for him to be happy and to have a chance at love again. She felt bad for her daughters but was resolute that they would survive. *"I'm disappointed that we grew apart—that he wasn't the 'love' of my life."* For a split second after one phone call to Frank, she considered going back to her family, but then she *"came to my senses."*

At this point in time, Dana was the most optimistic she would ever be. There was still a joyous naivety about her; she finally was in a place where she felt at home and she felt that her life was about to blossom. *"The streets and stones and buildings and river and people of my kind wait for me there,"* she wrote in late August. She said that her wings were completely formed and strong, ready for a jump from the cliff. She had just turned thirty and was looking forward to the next thirty years of her life.

New Orleans certainly seemed to suit her. Of all the places she lived, this was the best fit. The old buildings spoke to her, whispering a shared history. She felt as though she had traveled its ancient streets before in some other time, some other life.

To Dana, the power of the place was real, and its magic teased her into staying.

In one of her entries, she described putting her hair back in a colorful scarf and taking a walk. Along the way she stopped to buy a basket of ripe peaches. She absolutely must have looked as though she belonged there.

Frances once told me that she believed that she and Dana were in New Orleans together in a previous life. I forgot the particulars of her story. It could have been a dream or a tarot card reading that she had years before. But I vaguely remember the ending wasn't a happy one. Just like this time around.

Dana always summed up the prior months in the last pages of each journal, devoting a paragraph or two to the people in her life. For the man, Fritz, she wrote: *"What is he? Who is he? An unforgettable force for all time. I am deeply affected. I am deeply moved. I can't imagine I won't be for all time. In my heart where there was a hole—there is now him."*

As with the others, her relationship with him was fleeting. By the middle of September, he was gone from her life. He would reappear in later journals, but only in passing. Taking his place was a younger man she called Talon; she also referred to him as the "little boy" or simply "the boy." On September 20, Dana wrote that she was unsure what happened between her and Fritz. "*He just can't handle me. Oh well, I guess he's just not worthy.*" She referred to Talon as completely annoying. "*I shall probably attempt to first discard him within myself and then in reality.*"

By the end of October, she mentioned nine men that she was interested in or who were interested in her, and wrote, "*I want so desperately to be loved and cared for.*" Her worst fear was being alone and unprotected, and while she insisted that her "*freedom is the sweetest drink I've ever tasted,*" her one true desire was to find someone who would love and take care of her. While being on her own for the first time in her life was exhilarating, she never truly wanted to be independent. This was the place where she believed she would find the "*he that is to be the one.*"

She may have been preparing to divorce her husband, but she was already looking for this new and promised relationship. She was certain that he would be someone to love and care for her. He would be someone sensual, romantic, adoring, wealthy. He would be everything she insisted her husband wasn't. It was the relationship she believed she was destined for since she was a teenager.

Despite the exhilaration and euphoria New Orleans brought to her life, Dana spent the autumn of 1993 struggling with loneliness and depression, at least in the pages of her journal. Much of it was centered around her children. "*Welcome to real loneliness,*" she wrote on October 7. "*I have an urge to go scrambling back—reclaim my household and my children. What would happen if I did?*" And on October 21, "*I can't see from the agitation. Pain and agony regarding the children. How long and difficult this is going to be.*" And yet, she pushed the pain aside and stayed. She stayed because, again, she fully believed that she deserved to be happy and that New Orleans held the key to her destiny.

Outwardly, she spent her time with a growing list of people—tarot card readers, followers of magic. Most of them were men. She wanted another lover, and another relationship, the perfect man. Someone to adore her, worship her, lavish her with gifts. She wanted the impossible.

In these early days in New Orleans, Dana wrote vividly of the city. As the years went on, her writing became much more insular, drawing mostly from her thoughts rather than the outside world. On Sunday, November 7, at 4 P.M., she wrote that people passed her by on foot or on bicycles, "*not even aware they are captured forever by my words.*"

Although she was struggling with a loneliness that could not be filled by a casual relationship, she believed that her intensity intrigued, attracted, and could even repel, depending on what she wanted to portray to the outside world. *"Anything could be inside me—ANYTHING! Murderous imbalance, genius, idiocy, happiness, despair, talent raw or brilliant depending on the keen perception, or lack of it, from the humans who take that single moment to stop and look, <u>really look</u> at me."*

With her fingers cold from the chilly morning, she wrote, *"I am aware of the sunlight as it creeps up the Pontalba apartment building, fat strolling, over-zealous clowns, an oblivious tourist—layered over a background of mediocre blues and police sirens."* This was now her world.

Three days later, she was in love again. Enchanted, she said, *"I can barely look at him or speak to him. . . ."* She called him wonderful. He called her beautiful. It was like being sixteen all over again. His name was Aaron. As was the case with the people in her life—men in particular—there was no introduction to who he was or how she met him. He simply appeared on a page as her new lover.

In November, Dana took a bus to Pensacola to visit her children and, while there, missed this new lover even more. *"What has he been thinking? Has he missed me? Does he really want me? I want to hear words of reassurance."* This type of second-guessing a new relationship was no different than when she was eighteen and had just graduated from high school. Outwardly she was a grown woman, but emotionally Dana never seemed to move past being a teenager.

She was worried that the whole thing was imaginary, that when she returned to New Orleans, this man and his love would be gone. But that wasn't the case. This new "family," Aaron and others, made her feel welcome and loved—for a short time, anyway.

And in another rare moment, Dana seemed genuinely happy.

"I'm having one of those moments of solitude that I'll remember for the rest of my life . . . here with the sun streaming into my lap and on to my page . . . crisp morning . . . Remember the 'all is right with the world' feeling today—clutch it for the dark times."

This new, strange life made her feel electric, as though she was living in a dream. But she also felt vulnerable. On the Winter Solstice, 1993, she wrote, *"Who am I now? Who?"* She was certainly at a crossroads and felt her old life slipping away. "... *my children and all that is lost ... how strange this is ... how strange, all of it.*

Dana tried to dissect her relationship with Aaron. She loved his touch and the way they made love and the fact that he brought her flowers. But she wasn't sure it was love.

She enjoyed him, and she felt a comfort in New Orleans. But she still yearned to travel to England. That awkward teenager from Ohio, the young girl who lived her life through books and never felt as though she fit in, was still so much a part of this new, edgy, witchy Dana.

On a morning late in December, she stopped by St. Louis Cathedral and asked Mary to bless her children and bring them back to her. She sat in a pew and allowed the quiet solitude to wash over her. She asked for guidance, for protection and for success. She prayed to all the goddesses she knew: Frey, Freya and Mary. One of them surely would hear her prayer. "*Mary, Mary Dear Lady, smile on me.*"

Dana greeted 1994 still relatively happy with Aaron but missing her children. She also needed a better job because she hadn't made enough money in New Orleans to support herself. She complained that she would probably end up in the restaurant business again.

In early February she wrote, "*My children hurt tonight. I miss them and their touch and cuddling and I want them.*"

Although she was worried about her weight and didn't much care for her living arrangement—she and Aaron were staying with some others, including a man who was considered New Orleans' master palmist and card reader—she was getting by, looking forward to several new writing projects and her first Mardi Gras in the city.

Mixed in with all this, she was also writing about perhaps having a child with her young lover. "*I wonder ... will I do that? Would I?*" she wrote on February 4, 1994 about having another baby.

When Mark and I first talked about her entries pondering wanting to have another child, he was furious that she would even consider this. "Dana left her daughters to escape the responsibility of being a parent," Mark explained. For my brother, the anger was still fresh decades later because he lived through the wreckage of what her two children went through and how she destroyed her family.

In reading Dana's description of Aaron, I felt as though this young man was a decent guy, and, according to Mark, he was. Dana had a "type,"

PRETTY POLLY | 67
guys on the fringe, he explained, guys who didn't treat her well. Aaron

guys on the fringe, he explained, guys who didn't treat her well. Aaron was not that guy. Mark visited Dana in New Orleans, and he remembered Aaron as being a kind person, and Mark saw how Aaron helped her care for her children when they visited the city. Mark really liked him and wondered why Dana would have even given him a second thought.

In the spring of 1994, Dana and Aaron moved into what Mark described as an impossibly small apartment. Once living together, she wrote, "*I want to clean and do laundry and be happy.*" At this point in her life, she believed that Aaron was the "he" she waited for forever. "*It seems like old times in some ways. I watch him and wonder what shall become of us. I wonder if we'll last. I wonder if it matters.*"

She also began reading cards on Jackson Square.

Dana wrote many times of having a special power; not only did she feel she was unlike other people, she believed that she wasn't even a person:

> *I firmly believe that I am an integral part of the fabric of the universe . . . that my ideas and my choices shaped the way things are. No one else is imagining or pondering these things. To them, they don't matter. For me they are of crucial importance and I have always felt this way.*

When I allow myself to succumb to the romance of New Orleans and sidestep the reality of my sister leaving her family to pursue happiness, I daydream about her sitting at a small table on the square reading tarot for twenty or thirty dollars for tourists visiting the city. I wonder how many photos captured her image and what drew people to her. Somewhere, in a drawer that holds a photo album of mementos of someone's vacation, there she is, with long dark hair and intense green eyes. Polgara, a reader of cards, teller of fortunes, spending her days surrounded by the cacophony of jazz, blues, strolling minstrels, and storytellers. She was always very aware of how she presented herself. I often try to imagine my sister, now Polgara, turning over each card slowly and explaining to the person opposite her their possible meaning.

There she sat, waiting for those who needed to learn something about themselves. Perhaps they had questions about a lover or a job.

Maybe they wanted to know whether they would come into any money, or were troubled by a dream. Maybe they were curious about their future. I envy those strangers who were lucky enough to spend a half hour with her, and I wonder, more than anything, if those readings changed anyone's life.

CHAPTER 12

THIS LOVE WILL NEVER SAVE YOU

Dana, who wrote as a teenager that she was bored with the norm, found that her relationship with Aaron was much too serene. Just like Pretty Polly in the song, she gravitated to someone darker and more sinister, and by the time she realized it, it was too late.

Frances came to visit Dana in the spring of 1994, and, as visits went between the two, it was fairly civil. Dana wrote a lot about her children during this time and that sometimes she felt as though she *"ran away from home."*

"I miss my children terribly . . . more than I thought possible sometimes. I wonder if I should go back. I'm beginning to lose myself. I'm beginning to feel myself slip away into nothingness."

For the first time since she went to New Orleans, Dana's writing was completely focused on her children. She seemed genuinely worried about them, and, at times, her entries were tinged with regret. But, just like every other part of her life, she always seemed to embrace a thin thread of delusional optimism. *"I want my daughters to experience pride and self-satisfaction. I want that for them very much. I need to remember that I'll be their mother all their lives . . ."*

Later that spring, Dana went to Pensacola to visit her daughters. She wrote that she never wanted to be married, and she hoped that they wouldn't hate her when they were older.

Frances on a trip to New Orleans to visit Dana.

In May, Dana declared that Aaron was the "he" that she had been waiting for forever, but by July she wrote, "*Aaron is gone and then there is John Morgan, who claims to have the world in his hands for me.*"

He would change everything.

Dana first mentioned Morgan not long before she traveled to the Czech Republic in the summer of 1994 with a man called Stefano. She met Stefano in New Orleans, apparently, and was involved in a writing project for him. Dana may have also been romantically involved with him, but there was nothing indicating such in her journal. There is also no mention of why she traveled to Europe, whether he paid for her airfare, where she stayed, or what she did there. This struck me as odd, knowing how much Dana yearned to travel. Many of her earliest entries specifically mentioned her constant desire to go to England and Scotland. Certainly a trip to Europe would be important enough to share with her journal, but there were no entries offering any sort of explanation.

I remember that Frances, not long after I found her, gushed over my sister traveling to the Czech Republic to write a book.

There was nothing in her journal about the trip, about the place, its people, the cities, the countryside. This person who wanted fame and thrived on attention barely said a word about this project. But Dana did go on at length about missing John Morgan. He even called her while she was there. During the flight, Dana wrote that she desperately wanted someone to take care of her, and this someone now seemed to be John Morgan. She described Morgan as capable, stalwart, reliable, dependable, always caring, and always there.

Morgan was already changing her—even before the trip.

While Dana continued to record the scenes around her, sitting on Jackson Square while writing of *"the comfort of the breeze and the lovely red haired girl tap dancing,"* for the most part her entries reflected on what was going on in her head. These thoughts were obsessively devoted to Morgan.

Morgan seemed to be conjured from thin air. He was a part of that circle of tarot card readers and other followers of magics familiar to Dana. As she had done many times, this new lover completely captured her attention almost instantly. In October 1994, Dana wrote that she found it amazing that Morgan had been in love with her since October 1993. The journals made no mention of him, so I was unsure if she had actually ever even talked to him by then. Dana relished falling in love and reveled in the rush of a new relationship. Perhaps that is what drew her to him. She dwelled on two things: the security of love and the security of money. He apparently promised her both.

Not even two months after insisting that Aaron was the "he," she called him a *"lovely child who could never take care of me."* Aaron could offer her nothing. He was of *"no real value"* to her. *"I must throw my desire at Morgan."* And she did. Her feelings for Aaron soured. *"No magic,"* she wrote, and *"[Morgan] is so attentive."*

Amazingly, all of this transpired while she sat in a hotel room somewhere in the Czech Republic. There was a complete change of heart; Aaron was nothing but baggage to be discarded. *"Fights and more fights. I will be glad when it's done,"* she wrote in mid-August. She wanted the relationship to end amicably, and she thought that maybe they could be friends. She was sad but felt that her future was very bright with Morgan in it. She insisted in the pages of her journal that if she was in love with anyone, it was Morgan. She spoke her last words to Aaron on August 18 as he was leaving New Orleans for Texas, and wrote that, from that point onward, only the mailbox would be their link in communication.

While she was in Europe, she believed that Morgan was making plans to take care of her and wrote, "*he is getting a little castle ready and awaiting my return.*" She had always wanted a fairy tale relationship and now she believed that she had one. Morgan told her: "*Dana, sweetheart, how you always wanted a knight, well, darling, you have one now. Now and forever.*" He also wanted her to know that money was no object. "*Some day Morgan will be a hero and I could be that hero's wife,*" she wrote. She truly felt he could give her anything.

By mid-August Dana was certain of her choice. "*I will have all I desire. My book. My children. My future. And because of my choice to stay and maintain, I will build a future here. I have more faith in the possibility of my future than ever I have before. Morgan urges me gently forward. He has gently shown me that I can and will be all things.*"

Dana felt that her time had arrived, and despite not knowing him for very long and still not divorced from her husband, she had already contemplated marriage. On August 23, she wrote that he was the "*gateway to my dreams,*" and three days later, she expressed her love for him. "*I truly believe at this moment that we will be together forever.*"

Dana believed that she had finally found her mate. "*There is a beauty and certainty to everything in my life now. It's as if destiny thrust itself upon me with total clarity. I cannot and will not resist this. I am truly in love. All my lessons are learned and I am ready to reap the seeds I have sown.*"

She wanted to live out the Knight, the Lady, Courtly Love: the fantasy life that she imagined in the pages of her journal. "*He is my knight and my Lord and I truly believe at this moment that we will be together forever.*"

None of it was real. The relationship was already toxic.

I believe that she was aware, even in the beginning, that this man wasn't who she fantasized him to be, even as she went on about being so much in love and wishing to marry him and be with him forever. She had plenty of uncertainty, but she pushed it aside. She wrote of "*Walking rigid lines*" and meeting "*requirements.*"

Morgan was already shaping and controlling Dana so subtly that it was almost imperceptible. In early September she said that Morgan's "*anger and aggression seem very odd.*"

Although she believed that Morgan was the "he," she was also already questioning her judgment. Her initial reaction was to run, and that she felt this way astounded her. "*I will force myself to wait until the madness inside me passes. <u>Inside</u>, that's always been the trouble, eh?*"

Dana had a disagreement with Mark in mid-September over Morgan, his beliefs, and his excessive influence over her. But nothing would change her mind. Mark didn't like Morgan, and of all the relationships Dana had, this one puzzled him the most. He couldn't fathom what she saw in him. On September 12, 1994, Dana wrote, "*So, my brother—who has little to offer, feels the need to chastise me about my Morgan. How little he understands. I mean, what has <u>he</u> done for me lately? Not even the effort for a birthday card or gift . . . Morgan helps me with my pain. What is so wrong with that . . . he is my dream . . .*"

In the span of three days in mid-September, she penned troubling and bizarre entries.

She admitted that if something "*were to take him from me,*" she would choose to die, and she even knew what she would say in her parting note: "*But for my love of Morgan life is nothing. Without him I am more than lost and I shall join him.*" She also wrote about her willingness to allow him to kill her if they couldn't be together. At the same time, she was questioning her faith in him. As the months passed, she would pledge her love on one page and curse him on the next.

The day before the autumnal equinox, he was to "marry" her. Instead, they tripped on acid and he fell asleep. Of course, she couldn't marry Morgan in September 1994; she was still married to Frank. Just after midnight on September 23, 1994, Dana was distraught: "*I don't know. I'm confused and hurt and tired. And I'm not sure of my faith in him or any of this. I don't really want to go through all the shit it would take to make him 'sort of' understand my feelings. Just keep my mouth shut and play the game? I guess so. I guess so.*"

Several things would come to define this relationship. The first was their heated arguments. During the eight years they were together, Dana wrote of dozens of confrontations, and many turned physically violent. There were times when she counted days between fights, amazed when they managed to not argue for three weeks.

The second was their shared belief in the Norse religion. When Dana initially began her journey into Wicca in 1992, she seemed to gravitate toward Norse religion and mythology; this may have been why she was instantly attracted to Morgan. But again, there were no clear journal entries. She never wrote anything substantive about this chosen path until she began a relationship with him. Over the course of several years, Dana wrote that she was working on a book project based on two Icelandic manuscripts from the thirteenth century and the main sources of Norse mythology—the Edda. Dana indicated that she even had a title for it: *"The Girl Who Spins the Edda."* Like so many of her artistic endeavors, it was never finished.

The third and most lethal connection the two shared was their eventual heavy drug use. Later, Dana would write that it was drugs that bound her to Morgan.

The first months with Morgan were a marked change from other relationships. While she was over the top expressing her love, much as she had done in prior relationships—*"He is the universe to me. He is everything,"*—any stability was short-lived. Their relationship was volatile from the very beginning.

By October, Dana was already questioning its viability. Morgan, at times, made her feel complete, but there were other times when she perceived an *"empty wanting space between us."* She wasn't sure she believed her own heart. *"Do I believe 'the truth' is what he portrays? Do I really trust him and myself?"* In mid-October she wrote of being in the thick of *"another fight with Morgan and my patience wears thin. These get very, very tiring."*

She admitted, though, that even in her rage and irritation, she didn't want to leave him, and she was surprised that her tears didn't soften him: *"That does concern me, because they weren't a ruse. They were real."*

Morgan acknowledged during an interview with police in 2008 that Dana had a temper "which resulted in yelling and screaming arguments that were not physical in nature." Her journal entries would claim otherwise.

In mid to late October, Dana reread her early journals and jotted down passages from many of them. Perhaps it was a way to justify that she was destined to be in this place with this man.

In November 1994, she wrote that Morgan cared for her *"but at a great cost,"* and she felt that he had a way of making her feel punished or reprimanded. It unsettled her, and she tried to think of what she could have done wrong to elicit such a reaction from him. *"It's tiring to feel as if I must constantly watch my actions."*

Later in the same entry, she added, *"I feel as if all women invariably sell themselves to men and perhaps I have sold myself too easily."*

Her entries on November 21 and 22 were centered around her loneliness and sadness. The bliss that she wrote about during the very beginning of their relationship only a few months prior was completely absent as 1994 drew to a close. She was confused by Morgan and his treatment of her, and how, after only four months, he seemed to be constantly correcting her and not understanding her point of view.

But on November 23, Dana did a complete about-face. *"I'm embarrassed that I ever write that I could leave. I mean, who do I think I'm kidding? Where could I ever find anyone more devoted or perfect in every way? Who else would love me without fail?"* She said she was devoted unto death and that there was no turning back. Yet, two days later, she was again disturbed by something—she couldn't quite put her finger on it—that wasn't right with Morgan. She anticipated and longed for a closeness with him that didn't seem achievable. He was cold and callous, and she was very much unsure of a way forward.

This relationship should have gone the way of others in her life. In some ways, it had all the hallmarks of being the same. She fell in love. She grew bored and restless. She left to find someone new. But it didn't. Little by little, Dana realized—she knew—that Morgan wasn't what she wanted or believed she deserved.

Yet she stayed.

To me, the most perplexing part is that she stayed because she believed he was sent to her by the gods and that she needed to stay to fulfill some sort of divine promise. She wrote about this often, beginning when she was a teenager. She was emphatic that this was her destiny.

She worried about money. It would be an ongoing issue. She sometimes wondered why she wasn't with a rich man, because she believed that she deserved that in her life. Also, she seemed to always be the partner who had to hold out the olive branch. *"I am always the one forced to reconciliation,"* she wrote. And she observed that there was *"a coldness in him. A detachment."*

And yet, even this early in their relationship, she was afraid of being unloved, of being alone, and of being discarded. She always conceded. It was a never-ending cycle. It was this lack of confidence that kept her with Morgan. She constantly wrote of needing him to survive, to thrive, to find purpose and meaning in her life. She felt she was nothing without him.

In February 1995, after writing about the first of many times he hurt her, she continued to profess her love for him and her need for him.

She fantasized their marriage vows: "*We shall stand on cloth I have made on our rose petals—with candle light and our marriage certificate and my music and greenery, a wreath of yellow roses for my head.*"

A month later she was, once again, ready to give up. But not until she was able to "*correct my body.*" Only then could she leave. "*I am not the center of anything in his life. How can it be that I am so unloved?*"

Her divorce from Frank was finalized on April 19, 1995.

Dana and John Morgan.

CHAPTER 13

PERFECT STRANGERS

Dana and Mark had been exceedingly close for many years. But when Dana left her family, moved to New Orleans, and took up with John Morgan, the change in her was radical. So much so that it drove her and her brother apart for good. In 1996, not long after I found Frances, Mark and I talked about Dana's situation at length. I wanted to meet her, to know her. He told me that, at this point in her life, I wouldn't want Dana coming to my door.

Dana continued to spend her days as a card reader on Jackson Square and, with a journal always at her side, jotted down some of what she saw.
"A couple in love despite their children."
"An angry musician down on his luck."
"An accordion band."
"A hateful crone."
Dana created these written paintings at the end of the day after she had finished reading cards on the Square. Along with writing about this strange and freakish slice of humankind, Dana wrote about a girl from Cincinnati who stopped at her table for a fifteen-dollar reading. *"I wonder how many countless photos I'm part of,"* she mused.

She struggled to make a living, and in the margins of her journal she often added up all of her day's earnings and estimated what she would need for bills each week. It never was enough. Neither was the relationship. It wasn't enough and it didn't seem right.

Dana wrote that she felt as though she and Morgan were at an impasse and that they didn't seem to mesh. *"My personality grates him,"* she said in May 1995. *"What shall become of us?"*

Late May 1995 and through the rest of that year brought many changes to Dana's life.

In June, Dana visited her family in Dayton—it was a solo trip, no Morgan or children—and one evening during the visit, she, Mark, and Mark's wife, Kerrie, went to a movie together. Afterward, Dana stayed on at Mark's apartment for a few games of cards.

Dana was unaware that things were tense between her brother and his wife. This friction set the stage for an argument that would sever ties between Dana and her brother.

Something happened during the card game, no doubt having to do with the couple's ongoing quarrel. "It was probably something smart ass I said," Mark told me, "and Kerrie threw the cards." Mark doesn't remember what he said, or whether it was aimed as a dig toward Kerrie, but it was enough to send the deck spilling onto the floor.

Dana told her to pick them up, but Kerrie wasn't having it. Kerrie was angry at Mark and irritated that Dana would try and boss her around in her own apartment.

Kerrie told Dana to get out of her house. It was a mistake, Kerrie admitted to me recently. She said she was wrong to fly off the handle, and she told me that she was prepared to apologize for acting the way she did.

She would never get the chance.

Dana drove back to Mom's house and complained about how horribly Kerrie had treated her. Frances immediately left for Mark's apartment and confronted Kerrie, telling her she had no right to treat Dana that way. In the meantime, Mark drove to Mom's and argued with Dana.

Mark later told me that this person was not the Dana he knew. She had changed so much she was a stranger.

She and Mark had a huge fight that night—the crux of it over Morgan and how she was living her life.

During the argument Dana said she wished her brother dead. Dana would continue talking to Frances for nearly another year, but after that night in June 1995, she would never see or speak to Mark again.

On June 4, 1995, Dana insisted that someday she would cut Mark into little pieces. "*I curse you. I shall rejoice in your death. I wish death and harm . . . hear me, your life is nothing. You are dead.*"

It seemed that Dana was eager to have this argument, and she yearned for vengeance, believing someday she would have it. She wrote that her brother was disloyal and that his insults were still ringing in her ears. "*My heart feels completely unmovable where he's concerned.*"

Back in New Orleans, her relationship with Morgan was such a distraction that the days spent on the Square became tedious and boring. With her journal always nearby, she wrote often of how she wanted to go back to her apartment, and her focus was spent on wondering whether Morgan would stop by to see her rather than reading the tarot. She routinely counted the hours until she could take down her umbrella. Once very serious about her craft, she seemed bored.

The prior summer, Dana wrote of having a "*lovely and precious gift of sight. I have been called to share.*" That mindset was gone.

The mysterious Polgara no longer seemed as though she wanted to spend time offering her insight to others. Her mind was racing like a sixteen-year-old schoolgirl waiting to get a glimpse of the boy she had a crush on rather than what she purported to be, and yet, despite this obsession, she often wrote that the relationship didn't feel right.

On July 22, she confessed that she was hurting and alone.

> *I am as alone as I can be and he is without comfort for me. I am the center of the universe? Right. I am nothing. I believe in nothing. All I know is I'm fat and unprepared for what's to come and his dreams don't really encompass mine. All he wants to do is fight. War. He doesn't want peace with me. I feel horrible.*

As was the case over and over again, there were always prerequisites to leaving Morgan. She wrote that she wished to prepare herself to leave, however she needed to lose weight and write a book before she could "*gain my freedom.*" She still dreamed of living in Europe, "*as I always wanted. I'm dying inside.*"

From late July through early August, her journal entries expressed not only her boredom with Morgan but with potentially leaving him. On the one-year anniversary of their relationship, Dana felt alienated by Morgan. "*I think I'll go smoke dope. Gee, that's healthy.*"

Close to her thirty-second birthday, Dana hoped that he would do something special for her, and she was careful not to anger or irritate him. All the care to placate him was unsuccessful, though, and Monday, August 7, would prove to be a terrible day.

Dana declared that her entire life was held together by duct tape, and lamented that her birthday was "*horrific.*" It was the first glimpse at the direction of their relationship and the pattern of abuse that would become commonplace. Up to this point, there were many arguments and incidents of verbal abuse, but this was a turning point: the abuse turned physical. "*I cannot allow him to belittle me or call me names or shake me, or put his hands over my mouth, and tell me to shut up. He never talks about his fears or concerns. Ever. I'm bursting with worry and anxiety,*" she wrote on August 8, the day after her thirty-second birthday. The following day the cycle of forgiveness began and he touched her head and hair, rubbed her back, and then made love to her. "*Perhaps we will survive,*" she wrote.

Her children visited her for a week in mid-August, and Dana noted how strange it was to see her daughters. She said she was attached to one and detached from the other. "*Hurting and wanting it all to be over,*" she wrote. She was relieved, though, that for the time her children visited in mid-August 1995, she and Morgan didn't fight.

Her time reading cards on the Square was coming to an end. She decided that she needed a more lucrative way to make money. She thought that sex work would be the answer. "*My face is a commodity now,*" she wrote at the end of August. She was still disgusted with her body and she hated Morgan much of the time.

She detested her dependence on him.

CHAPTER 14

FLESH FOR FANTASY

By late August 1995, Dana was devising a plan to make lots of money, and it would be through sex work. She had high hopes for this business, writing that anyone who wanted exclusive rights to her would pay $8,000 a month.

Dana placed ads for her new business and then waited for the phone to ring. "*Ring phone,*" she wrote on August 23. "*Be a useful caller.*" She was charging $250 an hour, $400 for two hours, $1,000 for a night, and $2,000 a weekend. "*I see this as a clear, feasible and viable way to achieve my goals.*" She wanted land and a house. She wanted to live in the woods. This was a recurring dream, having a place of her own where she could practice her craft and write. She was certain this was the way to achieve it.

Dana had written often about how she believed she could seduce men. She described the way men looked at her and was fully convinced that they desired her. It is impossible to know whether this really happened or if it was a fantasy made real in her mind. As with many significant decisions in her life, there is no clue in her journals as to what made her commit to this new vocation.

Even with this chosen new path, Dana reluctantly continued to read on the Square because she didn't want to lose touch with that community and the clientele, but it seemed more frustrating than ever. On September 9, she complained that another reader was getting all the business. She wrote that when "*J gets a reading before me, I know the world is coming to an end . . .*"

On September 14, Dana described one of her sex clients, a man named Mike, as a "*strange lawyer.*" She indicated that her take-home from this liaison was $120. "*Rooms are horribly expensive. I need that to change,*" she said. "*More of the same tomorrow. Gordon.*" A day later she wrote that she and Morgan weren't getting along. "*We'll never make it. He doesn't make up for his mistakes and he pushes me too far. I must teach myself to not need him anymore.*" She said she was sad and angry and feeling hopeless. She also wrote that he hurt her again, adding, "*He is not right for me.*" She believed she deserved more and thought that perhaps she should work on her own goals. Her struggle with weight was front and center in her entries. She weighed 196 pounds.

By early October she weighed 188 pounds and declared that as she lost weight, she felt her confidence boosting. She jotted down her weight loss goals, which ended with a weight of 118 by May 1, 1996. Things seemed to be on track with Morgan again, and she mentioned that she and he would eventually be moving to Georgia. In mid-September, she and Morgan were sleeping apart, but by the end of the month, they once again reconciled and she wrote about how close she felt to him.

As would become routine days after their fights, her entries described how wonderful he was and how much she loved him. And on October 5, she bought him a present, a Remington 12-gauge 870 Model pump shotgun so he could go hunting.

After several entries of complaining about the relationship, his self-ishness, and how she doubted Morgan even understood romantic love, she declared: "*How can I even begin to explain the past day? Never, ever has it been this good between us.*" Dana said she was overwhelmed, enchanted, bedazzled, and awe-struck by him. "*It was like the sweetest breeze blew through our lives.*"

This bliss lasted until November 3, when she called him a clod. Nonetheless, she settled into a relatively quiet routine with him, jotted down her weight goals again, and, on November 13, wrote that she and Morgan were getting along well and had no fights.

Dana's new business was in its formative stages and she was frustrated that she had very little work. But she remained optimistic and was thrilled that she could "*develop relationships with men who genuinely enjoy my company.*" Even though her body wasn't yet perfect, she said the experience taught her that *"physical perfection doesn't necessarily mean an individual is a good sex partner, and that's what it all comes down to, doesn't it?"*

At the end of November, she gathered another client, Lincoln, which inspired her to consider writing her first book: *Memoirs of a Contract Courtesan.*

On December 9, Dana lamented, *"How many times in my life have I waited for the phone to ring?"* It seemed as though she was always waiting. Waiting either for Morgan to call her or for a potential client. There were dozens of entries focused on Dana's loneliness, boredom, anger, lack of friends and disappointment, and counting the hours when Morgan would walk through the door.

CHAPTER 15

COUP

After Dana left her family in 1993, her main contact with her children was through occasional visits. When Frances alerted her to potential issues and rumors regarding the mistreatment of her children by her ex-husband's wife, Dana was forced to do something. What she did, however, ruined any chance of a normal life with them. Led by Morgan, she also closed the door on any future communication with her mother.

On November 17, Dana wrote, "*It's amazing how much one call to my mother can affect/effect me. I worry very much about the children.*" This call caused the first domino to fall. Over the course of the next thirteen months, Dana's life—and that of her children—would be permanently altered.

Frances was worried about her grandchildren, and while Dana never wrote much about allegations of mistreatment in the journal, it did cause her to immediately follow up with a phone call to the preschool they attended. Dana was angry that the staff at the preschool wouldn't speak to her about her youngest daughter. "*I feel terribly upset inside in that place that eats at my stomach,*" she wrote, adding, "*They treated me like I wasn't entitled to information. They were unaware of my existence at all.*" She said that the school administrator treated her like a criminal. "*It was embarrassing,*" she said of the phone call.

Dana also explained that her youngest daughter had to be taken to the emergency room twice and she was never told. "*I feel sad and worried now,*" and she was irritated at her ex-husband for not talking to her about anything. "*He is pretending I don't exist.*" She had absolutely no one to talk to. She was isolated even then; Morgan was her only companion. "*I need to work this out as calmly as possible and not be over emotional. Stop my heart from beating in my throat . . . the children were never harmed when they were with me.*"

Dana's ex-husband had remarried, and because Dana had been out of their lives for so long, it's difficult to know what she expected. The children's stepmother had taken Dana's place, like it or not. In her journal, Dana addressed her ex-husband directly. "*I've been gone for more than two years. You have been married since June, you have a child with someone else . . .* " Dana tried to convince herself that she was justified in leaving her marriage to find happiness, but she also worried that her children might hate her and that they would never believe that she even missed them. "*What are my responsibilities to them?*" she asked herself.

She had no idea how to proceed or what to do and so, for over two weeks, she did nothing. Not only didn't she do anything regarding her daughters, she didn't mention them once in her journals. Instead, she wrote that she was bored, that her business wasn't going as well as she had hoped, and she continually tried to dissect her relationship with Morgan, which, on any given day, could be either unbelievably incredible or absolutely horrible. There was one constant, though. In every journal entry, she fretted over her weight.

The subject of her daughters would return to the forefront in a lengthy entry on December 6, and in it, she wrote, "*I miss my children today. Someday, some years from now, I shall share these few lines. How I wish I could help them. I'm not quite sure if I'm ready to have them or not.*" She said that she never wanted either one of them and insisted that she did what she could for as long as she could but needed to leave the life she had—one of pain and loss—so she could find happiness.

It seemed to me that it was always about her happiness and not that of her children. Ever. Then I remembered what my brother and his wife told me: Dana was a good mother. I wonder what happened. So many of her journal entries expressed her dissatisfaction with motherhood, and at times, she seemed to despise it.

On December 8, she said that her heart hurt over the children and what allegedly was happening in their lives, but that her duty—her responsibility to them—was unclear. Her children did, however, become front and center in her journal entries by mid-December. She asked herself whether she could win this fight, only guessing that the fight meant legal proceedings to grant custody to Dana. She said that her ex-husband, from the beginning, had *"dictated and threatened, intimidated me at every turn. No civil words. No chance to speak to each other."* She also alluded to a court deposition—perhaps to decide on custody issues—where Frank apparently told the court *"that he would prefer I never see them."* She called his words *"amazing and foolish."*

On December 19, she wondered how many days she could keep the children on a temporary order. *"Do I get to speak to the judge? What if I lose?"*

She wrote pages about possible options and believed that *"now is the time to fight for them . . . They should turn them over to me."* She was hoping that Frank would simply relinquish custody to her, but she also seemed ready for a fight. *"I must do what I must do and I believe the time is now,"* she wrote on December 21.

In December Dana had the children for a week on a court-authorized visit. She vowed that she was going to start taking care of them *"because they're mine and I believe I'm ready now. I want to be their mother."* She had also been devising a plan to simply keep them, sorely underestimating her ex-husband and what he was willing to do to stop that from happening. *"All about to transpire. My plans are as well laid as they can be. I don't think he'll buck me because it would cause him so much trouble. Either way I have a plan and once I get them here he'll have a real hard time getting them back,"* she wrote on Christmas Day.

I wonder how much of this plan was devised by Morgan and where she got the money for an attorney, which would not have been cheap. I'll never know if Morgan gave her the money, or Frances, or if Dana had saved some from reading tarot.

On December 26, Dana took a flight to Dayton, Ohio, to pick up the children. She arrived in New Orleans with them the next day. She was determined to *"make it alright for them. Money and lawyers and all set right."* She also wrote that she finally felt in control of her life for the first time in years. There were no entries until January 2, 1996, when she admitted: *"Many strange days in a row and I'm distant from the man I love and feeling, who knows? Trying to adjust to all this."*

When the week was up, Dana kept her daughters, and her ex-husband received a letter from Dana's lawyer informing him that the children would remain with her because his new wife had been beating them.

The charge set off an investigation by social workers seeking to know if Dana's daughters had been abused by their father's new wife.

"Child Protective Services was all over them and nothing stuck," Mark said. On January 26, 1996, Dana waited for her attorney to visit after a hearing about the case. "*Wondering what happened in court. If I won,*" she wrote.

She didn't win the court case, and by early February—in an effort to keep her two daughters, now aged five and seven, safe from what she believed was an abusive home and away from their father and his new wife—she, the girls, and Morgan left New Orleans and went to Puerto Rico. It would be the first stop in nearly a year on the run. Rather than continue to pursue the situation through legal channels, Dana basically kidnapped her children. She had to know that whisking them away would not end well. Or perhaps she didn't. Maybe the ending to this story, in Dana's mind, was the stuff of another of her fantasies.

At the end of January, Dana wrote that she was feeling vulnerable and worried about the future, and she was frightened to leave. She was estranged from Morgan and she wished for some sort of closeness. She hoped for a miracle. "*Little felt these days as my life has no meaning to me anymore. Few pleasures—no respite. Sad. Wishing I were dead.*"

On February 4, in Puerto Rico, Dana wrote "*we have nothing but faith to live on.*" She felt at odds with Morgan and was troubled at how "*strangely strict*" he was with her children. She never described what she meant. That day's entry also was partially devoted to Jim Brown, her one-time lover whom she hadn't seen or spoken to in years. It was his birthday. "*Happy birthday, Jim. I'm sure you don't remember mine.*"

Dana complained of the lack of money, the lack of drugs, the uneasy state of her relationship, and her need to lose weight. She flat out said her life was fucked up, and she wondered how to get out of the situation. She prayed to the gods for things to get better.

"*I really don't understand us anymore. My life is pathetic. I have nothing.*" Each day's entry had three components: lack of money, her weight, and the state of her relationship with Morgan. As for the latter, it oftentimes played out like this: one day good, one day bad, one day endlessly in love, and the next ready to leave him.

As February came to a close Dana continued to wish for a miracle and prayed to the gods to make it happen. "*I need a miracle because I'm scared to death and feeling like the world is going to fall apart.*"

By the end of March, with no chance of making a go of things in Puerto Rico, plans were in place to leave the island for Seattle. A week and a half before the flight, she complained again about her relationship with Morgan. She called him a pig and wrote that she didn't understand him at all. She said that she was disillusioned with him and added, "*He has no emotion and I feel like I'm looking and waiting for something better.*" She also ranted about hating her life and never wanting her children, even though she wrote that she still felt love for them. Again she pained over her desperate need for money and the stress of taking care of her daughters. "*What I really want,*" she wrote, "*is to be free.*"

On April 5, 1996, the evening before they left San Juan, Dana griped that Morgan was "*acting like an asshole again.*" She wondered what would become of their relationship and called him hard and hateful, immature and selfish. As would be the case many, many times over the years, she vowed to leave him once she was thin. The next day they were all on a jet headed for Seattle. Dana had owned a German Shepherd mix named Lu when she lived in New Orleans, and the dog went with them to Puerto Rico. It's unclear whether Lu continued with them on the journey because, in an entry on April 6, Dana wrote, "*poor Lu. Someone help her.*" It seemed that she abandoned the dog in San Juan.

Shortly after they arrived in Seattle, Morgan was tasked with finding them a place to live. Dana wrote of a "*brutal, painful argument*" they had the morning of April 8. Even so, she admitted that she found herself needing him more than ever and she wondered why. By April 11, they were living at 1414 College Street, Apartment 1. She penned that she was mostly unhappy, due in no small part, to the responsibility of taking care of the children she insisted she never wanted. "*That I've done all of this to my life shocks me when what I really wanted was to be free of all that shit.*" She hated the responsibility of schooling them and being so constantly close to them, and then she cursed her ex-husband and his wife.

What happened next was decisive.

~~~⌑⌑~~~

At this point in time, I hadn't known Frances for even a month. Each day brought something new: a history, a family, a sense of self. It was overwhelming—an emotional avalanche. I had only begun to grasp who my birth family was, and I truly knew nothing substantial about Dana's relationship with her mother. While I was trying to take in all that was happening in my life, Dana was preparing to erase Frances from her life once and for all.

On April 12, 1996, at 6:30 P.M., Dana wrote that she felt she was at an end. Morgan suggested *"fucking [Frances] over—just escape from her too, and I wonder what my conscience can take. What is right?"* She pondered whether going forward with this plan would be enough to give her a new lease on life and new hope. That Dana's relationship with her mother was volatile was no secret. Dana wrote about it ever since she was a teenager. Frances could be cruel and overbearing, and she oftentimes inserted herself into Dana's life. But there is no question that Frances loved her daughter. Dana realized this better than anyone, and there were many entries where Dana wrote about borrowing money from her. Frances always obliged. This would be the final time.

On April 13, 1996, Frances's birthday, Dana—at Morgan's insistence—charged thousands on Frances's credit card and severed ties with her mother permanently.

On April 15, Dana penned this: *"So, I killed her on her birthday and as long as he will protect me—it is over. I was dutiful with never a reward. I was loyal with never an accolade. Nothing. And so I took it as far as I could and have obtained a certain wergild."*

The choice of this word, *wergild*, struck me. In ancient Germanic law, wergild is the amount of compensation paid by a person committing an offense to the injured party or, in case of death, to his family. So that is what Dana felt she was owed by Frances, owed because she considered herself the injured party.

She said she felt a strange victory and believed that Morgan respected her more for what she did and that it made them better friends. *"There's no turning back and I will not miss her or feel guilt for what I've done. I wish her never to touch my children or see her again. I remember, with pain and loss, how many times she failed me."*

One of those purchases, a coat, was her trophy.

"*I will always remember what it felt like to try it on and to want it and buy it . . . I like who I am. I like what I've become. I'm glad to be rid of her. Never to see her face again. Cleanse myself and be done with all that.*"

She listed her family and friends in her journal and crossed them out. She wrote: "*All gone. All undone. I am in control of my destiny.*"

She called Morgan her love, her hero, and her everything. "*What we are to one another can never be erased or replaced.*"

A month after Frances's birthday, Dana continued to revel in her act of vengeance.

"*Can you believe it? Never again to look at, talk to, be annoyed by all of them, those people who used and abused me. And I went out in style. I'm glad at what I pirated. It was deserved and I finally had my vengeance. They are gone and I'm so glad,*" she wrote on May 11.

There is no doubt Morgan had been grooming her since the beginning of their relationship. He pulled her away from her family and convinced her she didn't need any of them. Dana sold her soul to Morgan for $6,000 in charges on an AmEx charge card.

In December 1996, Frances sent me gifts and a card. Her inscription read, "*My Dear Daughter and family, May this Christmas be a special one for all of you. We have been blessed by God in finding one another. How can I thank you for wanting to find me. You have made a very sad year a happy one. One day you'll meet your sister and we'll all be a family together . . .*"

One of the most widely circulated photos of Dana on the internet. Frances kept this photo in her wallet.

CHAPTER 16

FINDING MY WAY HOME

American poet, essayist, and feminist Adrienne Rich, in her book, Of Woman Born, *described the loss of a mother to a daughter as a tragedy. As an adoptee, I suffered this loss. It is a loss that cannot be reclaimed. The loss becomes part of you as a person.*

When I was a senior in college, I wrote an essay for an English class about being adopted. This is the opening paragraph:

> *Somewhere along the way everyone's parents tell them of their roots. This is usually brought about by questions such as: What nationality am I? What country did Grandma come from? Was Daddy really a soldier? When I was young (four, to be exact) my parents told me I was adopted. And although I asked those same questions, and listened intently to the answers, I realized that this was not my history, these stories were not told to me by people with the same blood flowing through their veins as flowed through mine. I had no roots. I stood, not with a long corridor of history behind me, but instead, in front of a locked door.*

In the essay, I recalled a high school anthropology class where we were asked to draw a family tree. I wasn't going to complete the assignment, but I felt that if my parents found out, they would be hurt. I also felt that if I asked them if they knew anything about my history, that this would hurt them, too, so I said nothing. In my house, no one actually ever talked about my adoption, and I was always hesitant to even ask. It was taboo. My dad, in particular, would get very angry if I even tried to bring up the subject.

This seemed to be the moment in my life when being adopted ceased to be a novelty. I wrote, "*It wasn't until the emergence of Roots that I realized I was someone without any past.*"

By the time I wrote the essay, coping with being adopted was becoming more and more difficult. My questions piled up, and I wanted to know who I was. The lack of a past haunted me. I was amazed at how many references to adoption were included in my journals. I struggled with it, and I yearned to be given the opportunity to open the door, regardless of what might be on the other side.

The irony of this is that a year after I found Frances, my Aunt Mary Ann—Frances's sister—wrote me a letter responding to my request for family history information. She told me, "Imagine much info has been lost to us after this much time has passed. As far as I know, other members of the family have never shown the interest in our past members as far back as Italy. I'm not quite sure why your quest for this knowledge is so important to you. None of us born in the USA has ever shown an interest."

My Aunt Mary Ann was also an adoptive parent, and I wonder whether her daughter ever expressed an interest in finding her biological family.

It was late one evening when my mother told me I was adopted. It might have been my birthday. I was sitting on the floor in her bedroom and she was sitting on the bed. The walls were covered in Catholic symbols: pictures of saints, the Pope, the Holy Family, a crucifix. She believed that when the light shined just so on that crucifix, and it glowed, God was watching. She told me that my real mother couldn't take care of me so they were my parents now. That they wanted me and that I was special.

I had another mother. Really, how does a four-year-old process that?

And one time, when I was maybe ten, a woman came to the house for a visit. I really don't remember why; I had never seen her before, but I wondered whether she was my real mom—she had dark hair and dark eyes like me—and I wondered if she would take me with her. Maybe it was because she was young. My adoptive mom was always old to me.

She was nearly fifty when I was ten. We looked nothing alike. We were nothing alike. I always accepted the life I was given; it was who I was. I was an orphan being raised by two people who called themselves my parents. I was a blank slate.

After I turned eighteen, I sent a letter to Pennsylvania Vital Records inquiring about accessing my original birth certificate. My dad saw the letter and flew into a rage. He screamed at me, "She didn't want you! We wanted you! She gave you away! Why do you want to find her?" His anger was palpable and it not only frightened me, but it changed something in me. I felt as though I was their captive. The last thing they wanted me to find out was who I really was.

I often think of what Frances went through in the births of her first two children. With me, there was no joy, no flowers, no cards and well wishes. With Dana, she could only look forward to knowing that she didn't have to hand her baby girl over to a social worker and never see her again.

<hr>

In early March 1996, I was close to getting information about my birth mother.

My three-year search was coming to an end, or so I thought.

"I'm dead tired. The exhilaration—the emotional ups and downs of the past weeks have finally caught up with me," I jotted on a yellow legal pad. After a hiatus of over a decade, I started writing in a journal.

"I'm drained but still excited. My heart flutters at the thought of what has happened since Feb. 28. It's that date and yesterday—late yesterday—that will always remain so significant to me," I wrote on March 7.

Over the course of almost three years, I had exhausted nearly every available option in the search to find my birth mother. As a last resort I turned to a professional. This person, a private detective, reached through an intermediary. Known only to me as "HRH," he was able to do what I couldn't in three years. He had a name and address.

I took to keeping the phone right next to me every night, waiting for a call, hoping that he could at least provide me with some sort of lead. Late on March 6, my phone rang. "Are you sitting down?" he questioned. "Your case is done."

Unable to sleep, I picked up my journal. *"And now I wait. Wait for the answers to my lifetime of questions. Wait to hear a name, should circumstances have been different, that would have been mine. Wait to introduce myself to a family who may not even know I exist."*

I hoped beyond hope for a positive outcome.

Two days later I received a fax at work. I had a name and address for my birth mother in Alabama. I also had a phone number for my grandmother in Niagara Falls.

The information, when I finally received it, opened a universe of new questions.

I wrote: *"Now that it's in front of me, that I can see it, who I came from, it should be better. But it isn't. I still have no phone number for my mother. I feel so far away from Frances Nardine Galante, the woman who lives in Mobile, Alabama, and is supposedly responsible for bringing me into this world."*

Ironically, my biological grandmother was the first person in my family I talked to. I was anxious about making the call, but the woman on the other end of the line was pleasant. Susie, as she was called, was ninety and eager to rattle on about her daughter and the rest of the family. But I couldn't bring myself to tell her who I was. I just told her that I knew Frances and was trying to locate her.

After the call, I opened the journal again: *"For nearly 36 years I have been the beginning and end to who I am, and now I have a sheet of paper that says I'm related to all these people. It's almost traumatic."*

Unwilling to press my grandmother for a phone number, I sat down and penned Frances a letter and included several photographs. In my three-page letter, I didn't once write the word adoption. I told her that I had thought of her often, and I expressed my sadness at how circumstances can keep people apart. I told her a bit about my life, what I did for a living, my family, and some of what I found when I received my non-identifying information and some of what the investigator discovered. *"I know you were married after you left the Navy and have two children. I'd love to hear about them and about your life since after high school—the last time we were together."* I ended the letter with my contact information and told her I would love to hear from her.

On March 10, I wrote:

> *Well, I finished the letter I plan on sending. It'll go out in tomorrow's mail. She'll get it by midweek. And then what? Will she call and scream at me for disrupting her life? Will she deny being my mother? Will she return everything unopened? Expect the worst, so if it doesn't happen I'll be ecstatic. I am scared. I'm very, very scared.*

I waited.

I worried.

And I waited some more.

For my entire life, up to that point in mid-March 1996, I had no information about who I was. I was comfortably ignorant, I suppose. It was easy to fantasize about birth parents. They are always famous or rich or both. They are never ordinary people with ordinary problems, and so, going on with my life wanting to know but not knowing, I could be anyone that I wanted.

Finding a birth family changed everything.

On March 12, I surmised that the worst-case scenario would be a denial. "*I'm trying to prepare myself for something like that. None of this is yet real to me. They are names on a piece of paper and nothing more. I need it to be real. Frances must make it real for me.*"

My mother called and left me a message on the answering machine on Friday, March 17. When I heard it at 12:45 A.M., I asked my husband whether he thought I should call her at one in the morning. He replied, "Do you really think she can sleep?"

I made the call and we talked until 4 A.M. I talked to her on Saturday and again on Sunday. My next journal entry was simple: "*This is all so unreal.*"

She had no issue telling me about my birth family, or about my birth father.

She had stayed in touch with him all these years because she knew that someday I would find her.

Recently, for the first time in nearly thirty years, I listened to the cassette tape of her message. Unlike 1996, when it was the beginning of a new chapter in my life, hearing Frances's voice again was bittersweet. That message, some cards, a couple gifts, and a few photos are all I have left.

She recorded her message at 9:10 P.M.:

> *This is Frances Cela. I just received your letter and your pictures. I must say you are beautiful. I would really like to talk to you. I am not surprised. I had prayed so long that you would get in touch with me. I tried to find you for a long time but couldn't do it.*
>
> *Right now I'm in Mobile, Alabama. I work for Jerry's Caterers. I'm going to be moving to Clearwater, Florida. I'll be here for a few more days. I will try calling you again. Thank you so very much. You really made my day.*

By the end of March, my birth mother and I were settling into a pattern of communication. "*Sometimes it's comfortable,*" I admitted. "*But more often than not it's rather awkward.*" My mother and I were still strangers, and even though this woman gave birth to me, I didn't know her. I hadn't yet received a photo of her, so I had no idea what she looked like. She was simply a voice on the telephone telling me about her life and her family. My family. I wrote, "*It's like putting together a puzzle. But I'm only beginning.*"

My mother told me about Dana, that she and her children and boyfriend were on the run, and that Dana was trying to protect her daughters from her ex-husband and his new wife. I didn't know anything about Dana then, or that she left her family in 1993 and very rarely saw her children over the course of those three years. Not knowing any of this, I started a letter I would never send to the sister I would never meet.

> *Dear Dana,*
>
> *Hello to the sister I've never met. It's odd inheriting an entire family in one fell swoop. Even though I'd been trying to prepare for the possibility of brothers or sisters, it really didn't hit me until Frances began talking about you and Mark.*
>
> *I won't get the full impact until I can talk to you or see your photo. I'd really love to meet you—I'd love to meet everyone! But I understand things are tough on you right now . . .*

As the weeks went on, I talked to my mother every few days, but she was still very much a mystery to me. "*Sometimes I talk to her and it's like talking to an old friend. But at the same time it's so unlike anything I've ever experienced.*"

I struggled with whether to tell my adoptive parents. In the end I decided it would be a bad idea, remembering my adoptive father's reaction when I tried to search nearly twenty years earlier. "*I feel as though it will bring nothing but grief,*" I wrote in my journal.

I was still waiting for a photo, for the opportunity to meet my birth mother, for something tangible.

"*I'm having a difficult time processing all this information—all these emotions. It's draining. Sometimes I am simply exhausted.*"

Dana always seemed to be a part of every conversation I had with my birth mom, especially in the beginning. Frances loved her so much; her love for Dana was very different than her love for me. She once told my brother Mark that I would be okay. He would be okay. We were strong. Dana wasn't. Little did I know Dana cursed her entire family and there wasn't a chance in hell I would ever hear from her.

I sometimes wonder, what if I had found my birth mother when Dana was still in high school? What if I had tried searching for Dana despite my birth mother's insistence that she would turn up and warnings from my brother that maybe I didn't really need this person in my life?

Frances's grandfather Nicola Linza and his son, Joe. When I was doing family research, I discovered that Nicola actually worked in the mines in Elk County. He eventually relocated to Clymer, Pennsylvania, and years later moved to Niagara Falls.

Frances's mother (left) and father. The woman on the right is unidentified.

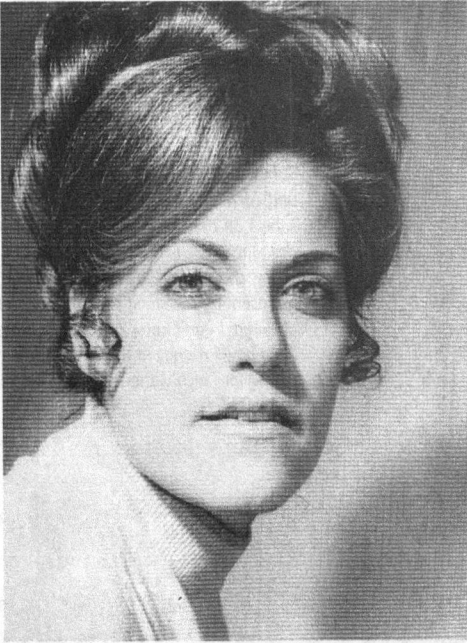

Frances in the late 1960s.

My birth father and me

I grew up in an area called Bennetts Valley, and each Labor Day a community celebration is held on the school grounds. Part of the day-long event is the crowning of Miss Bennetts Valley, chosen from a group of teenage girls representing the small towns that comprised the area. I don't know how I won. It could have been how I managed to eat the spaghetti they served for lunch without making a mess. This was 1977.

My first rock band, 1982..

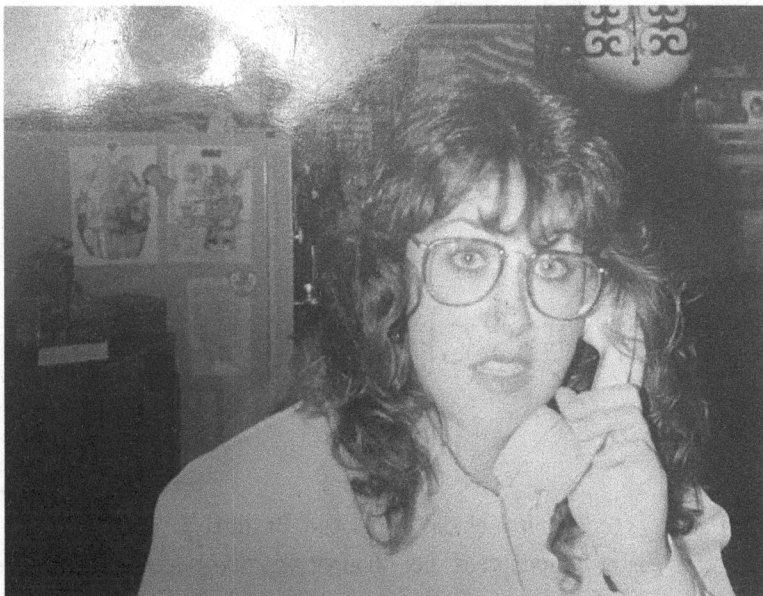

An undated photo of Dana.

Not long after I found Frances, she had this
Glamour Shot taken. I always wished she would
have included me in the photo shoot. I have no
photos of her and me together.

Frances circa 1990.

CHAPTER 17

MOTHERLESS CHILD

Poet Jan Beatty's adoption memoir, American Bastard, is frank, honest, and unapologetic. For many adoptees, her thoughts on the two words, family and home, are painfully familiar. Neither are happy words. And what of my home and my family? When I was young and visiting friends, I was almost in awe at the interaction between them and their parents, particularly their mothers. Nothing in my life resembled anything remotely close to that kind of bond.

When I look back on my childhood, I simply cannot remember any poignant or joyous moments with my adoptive mother. Regardless of how deep the dive into my past, I always come up empty because my adoptive mother and I had virtually no relationship.

I grew up in a house built by my adoptive father and grandfather, situated next to a small store and gas station operated by his family. It was across the street from the elementary school I attended and next to the ball field where I spent many of my summers. Though modest, it could have been described as almost idyllic. But the house was a shell. My adoptive mother was simply incapable of transforming that house into a home. It wasn't even how I felt, though it seemed sometimes that I was just a guest. She didn't leave an imprint. It could have been any place in any town.

It wasn't until many, many decades later, when my adoptive mom had been admitted to a geriatric psychiatric unit, that I even began to understand her. Even then, mustering empathy and sympathy for this woman who raised me proved difficult.

Following the death of my adoptive dad, she had a series of health scares that rendered her unable to walk. She spent time in a nursing home and then was transferred to an adjacent assisted-living facility. She truly thrived in this setting. The structure was good for her, as was the opportunity to interact with others. However, her mental health deteriorated to the point where there was absolutely no option but to have her admitted to the hospital for her safety as well as the safety of other residents and staff. As I discussed her condition with a nurse in the unit, I gained a much better grasp of who she was as a person.

I knew a few things about her past, mostly from overhearing conversations between family members. As a child, every Sunday afternoon was spent at my adoptive mother's homestead. There was always a roast chicken for dinner, and most of her immediate family was usually there for the afternoon meal. I don't recall it being a happy place, and, for the most part, I was left alone. To my adoptive mother's family, I most certainly wasn't a part of the clan. I still remember overhearing comments made by one of her family members. I was in the next room but close enough to hear. She said that I looked like a little witch with my unruly hair and that someone should really do something about my appearance.

I distinctly recall when her father died by suicide. I was about nine. He was found hanging from the rafters of the barn. Her parents also argued a lot and those arguments were sometimes violent. She had a long scar on her hand because she tried to keep her mother from stabbing her father.

I remember the nurse telling me that she had endured abuse as a child. The nurse never told me the details of the abuse, but she specifically used the word "horrific" in describing my adoptive mother's childhood.

My adoptive mom and I never discussed anything about her life. She was almost a stranger. But this episode, one that led to intense inpatient treatment, gave her the opportunity to release all the secrets she'd been carrying with her for nearly eighty years. She even told the nurses about a daughter named Marie, whom she and her husband adopted. That my adoptive mother knew my original birth name shocked me, and I wondered how many more things she knew but never shared. Not long after she was discharged from the hospital back into the nursing home, her severe mental illness, coupled with dementia, would take away nearly any ability to communicate.

For nearly ten years I visited a couple times a week, sometimes helping to feed her lunch or having coffee in the afternoon. She was best in the early afternoon. By evening, she would often drift off and say nothing. She had no idea who I was most of the time those last few years of her life, but, for the most part, she seemed fairly happy. She also began seeing family who had died. "Your dad is right outside," she told me during one particular visit. My father had been dead since 1999. In going through old paperwork stored in the attic, I came across something I wrote about her after a visit:

> *Mama sits and stares at the wall. Is she looking at something or nothing at all? Is she counting the days 'til death or remembering the adventure of her life? I wonder why they let her raise me. They didn't want to see that this was a big mistake. Nevertheless here I am, making her laugh, holding her hand and knowing that if she only could she would turn the other way.*

In March 2010, she became seriously ill, and I spent most of the last two days of her life sitting in a chair beside her bed. I talked to her, read her passages from books, sang her songs, and held her hand. I have no idea whether she heard or understood any of it or even knew I was there. It takes a lot for a body to die, even a very old and sick body. She died fourteen years to the day after I had first talked to my birth mother.

My adoptive mother was like a stone. She was bereft of emotion, and she was most certainly not like any of my friends' mothers. There were no sleepovers at my house, no birthday parties. Mostly, when I was young, I was embarrassed by her and her strangeness and her inability to carry on a conversation. She was a feral thing, insanely strong and convinced that someone was always listening, always watching.

She had weekly routines. She spent Monday doing laundry using an old wringer washer, even though my dad tried to convince her to get a new machine. She insisted a new washer wouldn't get the clothes as clean. Washing day was literally a full day.

So was ironing day. She ironed everything, setting the ironing board up in the living room with a clear view of the television in the parlor so she could watch soap operas—"stories," she called them.

Sometimes her hands would shake violently; sometimes she would weep. As a small child I had no idea what was wrong. When my dad got home from work, she would tell him that she knew this person or that person was talking about her.

Nighttime was the worst. More than once she woke up to what she believed were people outside the house. One time, she grabbed a shotgun and went out in the middle of the night to find them.

I still wonder what she was like when she and my dad met. She was a good-looking woman and he was a wiry young man with a mop of black hair. They made a handsome couple back in 1945. Regardless, he never would have left her in spite of her problems and their struggles.

I don't have many childhood memories of her. Nothing like the sentiments in Mother's Day cards. And maybe some of it was me. She was raising someone else's child, a child removed from her blood family, a child that was hers only on paper.

It's strange the things I do remember. One day we sat on the back porch steps and she painted my fingernails. Clear polish, of course, but that gesture meant something, and I still smile when I think of it.

One year, I gave her a bouquet of flowers for Mother's Day and she was thrilled by the gesture. I thought the gift was utterly useless except to bring about a little joy in her life.

Sometimes, on warm summer evenings, when my dad was working second shift, she and I took walks to my aunt's house. I liked her house a lot. It was bigger than ours, an old house with a cozy feel, and she had a dog. Those visits ended, though, when she and my mom argued over their father's watch. My mother insisted that it was promised to her in his will and that her sister had stolen it after he died. They didn't talk to one another for nearly thirty years.

Then there was the memory of something that happened when I was maybe four.

I must have angered her, but what I did at that age to make her so mad is lost to me.

I remember sitting on the kitchen floor, its big black and white linoleum tiles, tugging at the hem of her dress and crying because she wouldn't talk to me.

It's as though part of her wasn't present. There was silence and paranoia and mental illness behind it all. I remember my father pleading with her to get help and her staunch refusal. He was in tears. She screamed at him and took the pills the doctor had prescribed and threw them away.

He sat on the back porch steps and cried.

CHAPTER 18

TIRED OF RUNNING

It didn't take Dana long to realize that this adventure wouldn't resolve with a happy ending. The stressors of her relationship with Morgan were amplified when she was far away from anyone she knew, in a place that was strange to her, and in the role of twenty-four-hour motherhood, seven days a week. She complained in her journal that she was tired of having nothing and that her life at thirty-three years old was just as bad as it was at thirty. Always believing that the next thing would be better, they were off to Seattle.

Dana had high hopes for Seattle. She counted on money from escorting, finding new friends, and, of course, better drugs. But she also yearned for a full-fledged writing career, and she was truly convinced that if she wrote her memoir, it would be published.

The first month in Seattle was emotionally difficult for Dana. She relied more and more on pot to get through the days, and she still wrote something nearly every day about her weight. She felt overwhelmed, insecure, sick, and pained, and the paranoia over getting caught was constant. She wished for things to be better, and she wanted so much to simply sleep forever. *"It's like a horrible, expansive cloud of darkness hangs over me and I feel so hysterical and I don't know quite what to do,"* she wrote in mid-May.

By the end of May they had found a new apartment, and Dana felt as though things would finally get better. She put ads in the paper for new clients, and she mentioned several: Pete, Dwight, Mike, Dave, Jim.

A month later she added Chuck (who drove a Porsche) and Ron. Then Ron Number Two. And then Jay, with whom she became romantically attached. On June 16, she wrote, "*The most impressive part of the week was the take. Chuck $500, Sam $300, Ron $700. For a single evening. Keep it up, Polly . . . Money, money, money. I want money.*" And the money was good. "*If I had dreamed it three years ago, I would not have believed it. I am overwhelmed. $3,300 in three days.*"

Did she like the work because she found it easy to seduce men, because it made her feel beautiful, this once awkward girl who struggled with her appearance? Or perhaps it was something more. Perhaps, as an escort, she provided these men with a sensuality they craved but couldn't find in a relationship while she, in turn, was given the same.

It was as though her life was split in two. She was the mom who looked out the window of her rented house and watched her two young children play. "*So healthy, the blue sky, the puffs of clouds, the sun on my skin.*" And she was the sex worker who wore expensive clothes and was given lavish gifts. These things, the money, the gifts, were possessions she talked about wanting in her life. But from the notes in her journals, that didn't make her happy either. She was bored, even with the money and at least five steady, high-end clients.

By mid-July—only a few days before Morgan's birthday—Dana complained that she was frustrated with Morgan's constant job changes. She also was upset at how he treated the children. "*It serves to sputter our relationship,*" she wrote, adding that their union was strained. She believed that she was always the partner who tried the hardest in the relationship but that he never treated her the way she felt she should be treated. "*It's not enough,*" she insisted. "*Approaching 33 rapidly and I feel a fool.*"

On her birthday that year, she admitted, "*Sometimes I still miss my brother. I guess it's over. Sometimes I still get angry about our getaway, but I trust Morgan.*" How deep did that trust run, though? Later in the entry she called him an emotional cripple and said she felt wounded and alone. She found him to be crude and unpleasant and lazy, and, as with most of her birthdays, the day didn't live up to her expectations. She wished that her life could just be over, and she longed for peace in death. "*Wishing it were different. Sad. Blue.*" She wondered if she could ever be happy and she felt trapped. She called her birthday "*tainted*" and wrote that she hated Morgan, hated herself, and felt "*stupid for my choice.*"

Dana looked at most of her clients as business transactions. But one man, Jay, seemed to capture her heart. She met Jay on July 30, and it wasn't long after that she began to obsess over him. She wrote that she really liked him, and it made her feel like a teenager waiting for an invitation to the senior prom. "*He's what I dream about these days.*" She wanted him, not just as a client but as a lover. She fantasized about running away with him, and after he called her one evening, she announced that romance was in the air.

In August, Jay took her on a trip to San Francisco. She called it a surreal event. "*Neiman Marcus, a diamond bracelet, a watch, clothes, earrings, $2,000 in cash and a man who wants to be in love with me. My mind is spinning, reeling, and I'm trying to figure out what to do with him and my real feelings for him,*" she wrote from her hotel room at 12:45 A.M. because she couldn't sleep. "*Who am I now? Look at me, sitting in San Francisco in a $100 Dior nightie.*"

She was beginning to think of Jay as a way out of her relationship with Morgan, and wondered if Jay would end her struggle, and love and care for her. "*Would he really stand by me? Help me with my legal problems? To be saved, could it happen or would he prove to be worthless?*"

Did Jay ever give Dana any indication that he actually wanted a relationship—and not just an escort/client arrangement—or did Dana dream up his love for her? Nothing in her journal answered this question. The entirety of his attraction could have simply lived in her head. When she was frustrated with Morgan, she always looked for a plan B, and it typically involved a rich man to save her.

In mid-October, Dana announced that Jay was over but that he was sending her money. "*I pray my lords and ladies that it is a boon beyond imagination. Please let it be so.*" Three days later she received $700. She called it an insult and vowed to curse him on Halloween.

In late October, Dana was preparing to meet with a woman named Catherine La Croix. Very rarely did Dana give explanations about the people she wrote about in her journals. Most times she offered no last names, and other times she identified them only by initials. But a search of Catherine La Croix in Seattle revealed someone who would have been of real interest to Dana at this time in her life. La Croix was a former courtesan, porn actress, madam, sacred whore and pro domme, member of the Sex Workers Outreach Project (SWOP), and a Dianic Wiccan Priestess.

She was also the executive director and founder of the Call Off Your Old Tired Ethics (COYOTE) chapter in Seattle. In a 1996 *Internet Underground* article, "Love For Sale" by Tommy Ranks, she is quoted as saying: "Why is it illegal to charge for what can be freely dispensed? Sex work is no more moral or immoral than the chocolate or distilling industries."

Dana was hoping that she would be an ally and insisted in an October 22 entry that she was not intimidated. "*What's mine is mine. I did not need her to make me or my business.*"

On October 26, Dana wrote, "*so it would appear that Catherine has something to offer me. Now we must see how much there is to offer and what I'd like out of this. To have a chance to work and really make the money to take care of us. I'm sort of stunned and waiting for what comes next.*"

There was nothing more written of this woman in the journal, and by November, Dana was, once again, weary of life. "*I am unhappy as I can be. I hate my life and being trapped by my circumstances.*" She felt the gods had abandoned her, and wrote that she was bored and unhappy with Morgan. She called him "*mean spirited and emotionally stingy.*"

In late November she said she had nothing left, no hope or care. "*My life is bereft of inspiration or love. I care for no one, not even myself. I am hoping it will end. Perhaps I can find the courage to do it.*" In early December she admitted to being so sad that she could no longer bear the pain.

How much of Dana's real life mirrored these thoughts? Was it clear to Morgan and her small children that she was alarmingly unhappy, or was this Dana confined to the page? My brother, Mark, said he didn't recognize this version of Dana, so even if she was this distraught, she may have kept it hidden.

Dana wrote nothing for nearly three weeks. There were no entries about Yule, nothing about planning the holiday, or how she was going to celebrate it with her daughters. On December 26, she wrote that she loved no one and that she was consumed with anger and hatred. On December 27, Dana said she couldn't wait to die.

The new year began with this:

Sunday, January 5, 1997: *"Hello to a new year and to jail and facing Frank and court and endless days and nights without Morgan. But then there is back to New Orleans. Hopefully a party is waiting at the end."*

Dana's running was over. She was caught and arrested on January 10 and charged with two counts of child stealing. On January 15 she penned, *"I lost the children as I thought."*

There were *"tears and tears and tears,"* and she believed she had reached the bottom in her life. *"The pain is like glass. Broken and gouging my skin."*

Her case was heard in Ohio, as the children had been living there with their father and stepmother at the time that Dana was arrested. Mark thought that perhaps the girls were taken back to Ohio by law enforcement, but he wasn't certain. Dana pleaded guilty to the charges and waived the right to a speedy trial.

She was ordered to pay court costs and complete one hundred hours of community service. She was also ordered to obtain and maintain full-time employment. She was fined $1,000 and placed on two years' probation. Her father, who spent his career in law enforcement, helped her navigate the ordeal.

Dana always knew she had a father out there somewhere, but Frances never pursued visitation or even child support. Yet she may have—at least occasionally—kept in touch with Dana's dad.

I asked Mark about this, because it seemed so strange to me that Dana had absolutely no contact with her father the entire time she was growing up. Why didn't Frances encourage some sort of relationship between Dana and her father, especially when she was young? "Mom wouldn't hear of it," Mark told me. "It would have also thrown Dad into a jealous rage."

Dana first talked to her father on October 13, 1992, when she was twenty-nine years old, and this relationship was tenuous at best.

"My father fleshes out and is becoming a real human. I am trying amidst the chaos of my mother to not attach too much to the event. I struggle to make my own place within the framework they have given me. I was bastard-born," she wrote on October 22, 1992.

Frances had always told Dana that she and her father had been married. Dana thought nothing of it because she had his last name. But that wasn't the case. Dana's father was married to someone else and had a family. "Mom didn't just have a skeleton in her closet," Mark said. "She had a whole graveyard."

In some of her journal entries Dana spoke fondly of him, but her goodwill didn't last long. In the end, she was estranged from him as well, writing that she was happy that both her father and mother were gone from her life.

With the court case lost and the children remanded back to their father, Dana was free.

CHAPTER 19

THROUGH THE EYES OF
A CHILD

The last time Dana saw her children was in January 1997. The ruinous result of her choices fell squarely on the lives of her daughters. Both were young enough that their memories were perhaps no more than shadows and scents. They were gone from their mother for good, and as the years went by, there was less and less for them to hang on to; she was a ghost even before she died.

> **mourn (v.)**
> Middle English *mornen*, from Old English *murnan*
> to feel or express sorrow, grief, or regret; bemoan, long after,
> also "be anxious about, be careful" . . .
> from Porto-Germanic *murnan* "to remember sorrowfully"
> Old Norse *morn-a*, "to pine away"
> "to die, wither."

How can you mourn when your memories of the person you lost are so broken and scattered that it is nearly impossible to string anything together?

What if almost all you know of your mother is read in true crime blogs and podcasts and television shows?

How is it possible to strip away all of the noise, the bullshit, and find that person, no matter how damaged?

Dana's youngest daughter, in a blog from a decade ago, pieced together a picture of her mother from what little she could still recall. She wrote that she didn't remember how much of a mother Dana was but didn't hold it against her. She believed that Morgan had a lot of control over her mother, and she could recall Dana actually taking care of her in only a few situations.

She remembered playing dress-up and wearing her mother's makeup and looking in the full-length mirror that stood by itself near a large staircase in an apartment in New Orleans. She was disgusted by the cockroaches that lived under the refrigerator. The blue water and warmth of Puerto Rico were still vivid in her memory, as was the layout of the house in Seattle. She remembered eating green apples with ketchup at the kitchen table in that house, and she remembered laying outside her mom's bedroom door, pleading for her to come out and not getting a response.

She still feels bad for dropping and breaking a bottle of her mom's perfume, an accident that continues to embarrass her even after decades. "I used to remember the smell of it, but I can't anymore," she wrote. "That makes me very sad. It makes me long for the memory of the memory."

She was not quite five the last time she saw her mother. "She disappeared from me and I never saw her after she brought us back."

While she doesn't remember how much of a mother Dana was, she was no fan of her stepmother.

The kidnapping case was one of several featured in an article in the *Chicago Tribune* on child abduction. In it, the children's father and second wife discussed the allegations made against them by Dana. According to the article, the charge levied by her set off a full examination by social workers, including inspections of their home and mandatory psychological counseling that the couple insisted they never needed. Furthermore, their father's wife said that when the children were returned to them, they were emotionally volatile, rebellious, and suffered from sleep disorders.

Mark said that when Dana's eldest daughter was about eleven, she gathered her belongings in a pillowcase and told her father that she wanted to go to her grandmother's home to live. Dana's youngest daughter was placed in foster care and was also eventually placed with her paternal grandmother.

I stayed with Frances when Dana's youngest daughter graduated from high school, and I slept in Dana's room. Frances did her best to make the room inviting, and the bed was covered with a beautiful yellow quilt. I've only recently thought about how difficult it must have been for Frances to clean that room, the memories attached to it, the stinging absence. The room hadn't been used in years, and by the time I walked through the doorway, Dana was long, long gone.

Did Dana know when she closed her eyes each night and dreamed of escape that she would never set foot back in the place—the place where her daughter waited in cap and gown, looking so much like her mother?

CHAPTER 20

THE COST OF FREEDOM

Morgan made his way back to New Orleans while Dana sorted out her life. She was neck-deep in legal troubles, and there was no running away this time. She was charged in the Common Pleas Court of Montgomery County, Ohio, with two counts of child stealing, and she relied on her father, a man she barely knew, to help her.

Sometimes Dana's entries were more stream of consciousness than a description of events in her life. So was the case with the journal that began on January 8, 1997. She called this little blue book covered in fabric and tiny blue and yellow flowers "evil," because it chronicled the loss of her children, and she looked forward to running out of pages to write in it.

However, it also chronicled yet another relationship.

On that day, January 8, Dana was in Oregon on a bus back to Ohio for court proceedings, and in that entry she mentioned a man: Randy. Randy was younger, the same age as her brother, Mark. Randy was apparently a new love, a musician with long blond hair and a guitar, who said he could imagine a long relationship with Dana.

"His sweet face and voice, his warm touch and comfort. His tenderness and gentleness. His golden curls. His guitar. All music to my soul."

He appeared out of thin air. Maybe she met him in Washington, or maybe she fell in love with him on the bus. Was the bus a Greyhound, or was it transport for newly released inmates? There is absolutely nothing in her journal about how he came into her life.

"Shocking that I met Randy—an unexpected pleasure. His touch was sweet, yet powerful. Daydreaming of him is a nice distraction," she wrote on January 9, and on January 10 she wrote, *"Here with my father. Arrested today. So strange."*

In these beginning days of 1997, Dana wrote at length about how much she missed Morgan and New Orleans, and she was hopeful that he would find a place for them there to live once her legal troubles were settled. She was also distraught over the loss of her children. *"I find myself hurting because they are. I can see it in their faces."* She vowed to keep fighting for them.

Dana's father took her back to South Carolina to stay with him and his family for a few weeks. They arrived at his home on the evening of January 11, and she said she was glad, adding that it had a *"quiet, protected sort of feeling."*

Time moved exceedingly slow for her at her father's house, and a week later she called the passing of days weird and disjointed. She wondered what those who knew her in New Orleans would think of her when she returned.

On January 23, she had to see a court-appointed psychologist *"to have my head examined."* She was amazed that she told him that she was Polgara. *"To reveal is truly beautiful. I thank my gods and renew myself again."* Dana felt that in the blink of an eye, all her troubles would be over. *"I will be reunited with my love. The children and I will be restored to one another. The pain of separation will be over."*

There was no eloquent prose in this journal. Dana's words were choppy, fragmented, and disorganized. Her life was genuinely on hold and she felt lost and no longer herself. *"If only I could scream 'til it was out of me,"* she wrote on January 28. She would find herself saved only a day later, thanks to her father advocating for her, when she was free to travel back to New Orleans. She was ecstatic. *"So amazed I'm startled. Full circle . . . will it be like I never left?"*

The stay wouldn't be a permanent one, because Dana had to travel north again for more court dates. She was back at her father's in South Carolina in late February, and she wanted nothing more than for everything to be over so she could move on with her life. On March 2, sitting in a car at a rest stop just over the Kentucky border, Dana wrote, *"Only*

Frigga knows when and if I'll ever see my children again. Part of me wants to let go, forget, pay my child support and let time go by while I fix my life."

On March 4, she was back in Dayton for a court date, and she was upset that she had to travel back again in early May. "*The horror doesn't end and now my alliance with my father must continue,*" she jotted in her journal while sitting on the interior balcony of the Signature Inn in Dayton.

She was back in New Orleans by March 7, and her attention turned to Randy and Morgan. She loved the fact that she had a husband and a boyfriend. While she and Morgan never legally married, she often referred to him as her husband. Randy, the young man from the bus, with blond hair and guitar, was her new lover. It was an attraction that began in January and, by late March, she was anticipating his visit.

"*That I opened to him. That I want him. Strange and new. That I could love them both. That they could love me in return and that it could work. The idea thrills me,*" she revealed on January 12.

On March 28 Randy was at her apartment in New Orleans. She called their sex "*ho-hum*" but seemed to be pleased with him and called the company of her two men "*just grand.*"

But as would be the case over and over, she was again unhappy, detached, and feeling a need to run. "*I should be content, not having the financial worry. All that's in me feels like loss. I am less and less consoled by anything. So much wants me dead and gone,*" Dana admitted in a journal entry on April 4.

Dana continued to write about Randy—he had left New Orleans and wouldn't be back until June—and in a number of entries mentioned her children. She weighed the new freedom she had with the loss of their presence in her life. On April 19, she said, "*I smile at my life for the first time in a while. I'm so close to being what I want to be.*"

She had one final trip to make to Dayton at the end of April, and she wrote extensively about how much she didn't want to go. It would be the last time she set foot in Ohio, and I sometimes wonder whether she drove by her old home out of sheer curiosity.

She ended her journal before the trip north. As she did with all of her journals, she reviewed the time period it covered. She wrote about the loss of her children and her brother, but she didn't mention her mother.

On April 28, on the last page of the journal, she wondered where she would be in a year and asked that she and hers be kept safe.

Dana's father accompanied her to Dayton for the hearing. She took a bus from New Orleans to her father's house in South Carolina, and she and he traveled to Dayton together.

At the hearing, Dana was sentenced to two years' probation, ordered to complete one hundred hours of community service, find employment, and was fined $1,000. "*And that is their idea of generosity,*" she complained. After all was said and done, Dana wrote that it hurt to think she wasted two years of her life on this cause, but she felt she did the best she could. It was time to move on. She also wondered whether there was anything left to experience or discover in her life or whether living was simply an act of endurance.

On May 5, she left Columbia, South Carolina, and disclosed that her father had tears in his eyes at their parting. "*He's far more sensitive than he will ever admit.*" The next day she wrote from the Mobile, Alabama, bus station, excited about getting back to New Orleans and hoping that she was "*less than nothing to them in Dayton.*"

Back in New Orleans, Dana was once again preoccupied by thoughts of Randy. He sent her a tape of his music, and she raved about how lovely he sounded. "*I can hear his love and it's so touching to me,*" she said on May 10. She seemed satisfied, and she made a promise to take advantage of every moment and embrace her life in a way she hadn't before. "*Look long into my mirror and drink deeply from my cup.*" She felt protected and loved by Morgan and Randy and sensed a strength in herself that pleased her. And still, even with these entries that expressed a renewed hope, there was an undercurrent of sadness and fear. As much as she felt the exhilaration of this new freedom, her ball and chain was heavy indeed and, every now and then, reminded her of what she had left behind. These thoughts became more pronounced as the days went by. Dana was once again writing about her lack of focus and creativity. "*I'm so sad and bored. All the days run together like a string of dissatisfied moments,*" she told her journal on May 16 in an extremely long entry while sitting by the pool in the cool hours of the morning.

I don't feel like myself. I wait. I think about the past and have regrets. I try to sleep and sometimes I can. I'm so sad for all my losses.

I feel burnt and charred and full of no caring for anything. All that I ever wanted to say just choked up inside or jumbled up—not coming out in any useful order . . . I wonder how long it can go on. The days that will not end. The dawn that will not come. I feel at an end, as if I shall be dead soon. Or perhaps I am already.

Perhaps for the first time, Dana distilled her life into a few sentences. She was alone. She felt cut off from everything and everyone. She had no faith that her words could change anything. She was angry. She was the thinnest she had ever been, but for what? "*I need something I do not have, and I don't know what it is.*"

Ironically, being thin was one of her life's dreams. At this point she weighed 117 pounds. The mirror that once reflected a woman struggling with what she often referred to as an ugly body was now much kinder. She loved the way she looked and she wrote about it at length, as she did her strict regimen to keep the weight off. In her whole life she had never been this thin. She reveled in the size 4 leather skirt she could now wear. She felt beautiful and sensual and powerful. All of this seemed to tie into her irrepressible desire for Randy.

As May drew to a close, Dana wrote extensively about Randy. She was anticipating his visit and proclaimed a real and certain love for him. She believed that he never had anyone care for him, no "*good woman with any generosity or sensitivity ever touching or sharing.*" She called him "*bright and new and hopeful*" and said he offered himself to her in the most beautiful way.

Only a week before Randy's visit, completely out of the blue, Dana revealed, "*(Morgan) hit me in the face and bruised me. I don't know how I feel about anything. I guess I still love him . . . I guess I'll do my best to survive what must be survived.*" She believed that Morgan would strike her "*for mere words.*" She felt cheated in this relationship but ended up blaming herself for his actions. She said her face looked worse than it felt, and two days after the incident, she and Morgan talked and she forgave him. "*I know that I still love him. I don't know how to stop. It's he and I and whatever else comes our way. I still feel my duty calling.*"

Dana was counting the days until Randy arrived, and on her youngest daughter's birthday, May 24, she wrote, "*Six years ago today—my death. Today, my rebirth. I'm so glad I'm free of the past. Loving my little two bedroom, two room apartment."*

Did she truly believe it? After a year on the run, after doing whatever she could to keep these small girls safe, after her arrest, after multiple court dates, was it simply okay now? Okay that they were back in the situation she vowed to remove them from just a year earlier? Or was she trying to convince herself everything would be all right? Or had she simply given up?

Dana often tried to reason away the decisions she made. In the case of her children, she felt that someday they would be reunited. That thought was good enough, most of the time, for her to continue on with her life and not be crushed with guilt and loss.

She was glad that Randy would be there soon—she wrote with the excitement and newness of a teenager—but even with the pleasure those thoughts brought her, she didn't feel she could confide in him, or anyone, for that matter.

Once Randy arrived, those thoughts of a budding new relationship and the intense love she felt on the page dissolved into absolute nothingness. Only a week into his visit she was bored with him. She wrote that she no longer desired him and wanted to be stoned every moment of every day.

One of the most telling entries that revealed how Dana treated the men who came into her life, and how she casually discarded them, was written on June 2. "*So, everything changed with Randy. No sex at least until my birthday. I bet not at all. I think my attraction still holds but boy was he a fool. He has never given me a gift. I don't trust that. He would have to prove himself a great deal before I would consider him again for intimacy.*" She went on to say that he hadn't written her any letters or poems. "*Lover stuff,*" she called it. "*Tender words, gestures of kindness, self-sacrifice, consideration and respect. These are the foundation of love. He's too much a child. And Gods, do I want Morgan more now.*"

It was at this point she realized that she would never leave Morgan. Regardless of what happened between them, despite how badly he treated her, she emphatically believed, in her heart, that "*it all begins and ends with him.*"

It didn't take long for Dana to absolutely detest Randy: "*I look at him now and I feel nothing. Boy, I guess I can manufacture a lot within myself.*"

Perhaps none of it was ever real but rather a lingering teenage desire to be swept off her feet. The Randy she conjured in her head and in the pages of her journal never really existed.

On June 3, she wrote that he was in her apartment playing his guitar and that she couldn't "*give a flying fuck.*"

"*My love has turned to a queer hatred. What would have been so intimate before is now less than nothing to me.*" Dana had reached a point where she wanted Randy gone from her life. When she looked at him, she wanted to slap him. "*How is it that all can change so quickly? I feel a sickness sitting out here. I don't feel like I can manage it too much longer. I have an angry hatred in me. I hope he goes away soon.*"

Two days later she threw him out and proclaimed that she liked herself more for sending him away. She also pledged renewed love for Morgan. On June 7, Dana wondered what was going on in her head to want Randy to be a part of her life. "*I guess I felt I needed it, but Gods, what an annoying, weak piece of shit.*"

She declared that the past three years had been the best of her life and she was, for the most part, happy to be safely away from her past. "*Sometimes I feel like it's 20 years ago,*" she wrote on June 9. "*All the life I missed . . . returned to me somehow.*"

It didn't take long for the pendulum to swing in the other direction. By June 20, Dana was again unhappy with her relationship with Morgan and wrote that her children's hollow eyes haunted her in her sleep. Yet, she felt she didn't have the resources to help them and couldn't fight for them from New Orleans. Besides, the way she looked at it, it was no longer her fight.

All the fights in her life were with Morgan, and she was almost giddy in an entry in late June that detailed their brief breakup, him hurting her and them arguing in the street, only to reconcile later that night. The next day's entry was even darker. Dana wrote that she had dreams and nightmares of Morgan killing someone they knew "*just to see what it would feel like to have her offer her life to him, and then the macabre gift of the tiny black poodle and the comfort I received from my parents, new and better, and my fantasies about my own death at Morgan's hand. Several different scenarios flit through my mind.*"

But she also wrote about her children; they haunted her thoughts, their lives now so separate from her own. She was becoming accustomed to not having them but longed for their touch and their affection. "*How I wish it could all have been different,*" she wrote in early July. "*But it is not and wishing won't change it at all.*"

For the next four years, the duration of the journals, she would swing back and forth from being happy she was on her own to missing watching them grow up. She had bad dreams about them, and as so many times before and after the summer of 1997, she was unsettled, unhappy, and without any good friends.

The one consolation: she was a size 4.

"*I'm thin, beautiful, unencumbered, truly <u>free</u>. I feel like I don't have to look at my life with regret. And I've found him. The HE that was promised to me,*" she wrote in her journal on July 16, 1997.

Dana was isolated. She longed for one good friend but had none. When she did manage to build friendships, she found faults with each and every one of them.

Dana spent much of the autumn of 1997 trying to rebuild a life. She was hoping to land a singing gig with one of the local bands but wrote that she was stood up at the audition. She went to the Square to read cards, but wrote that the Square required a "*creativity and freedom of the mind I no longer have.*"

She continued to be cursed by the past, a past that no longer felt like her own. Yet, there it was, written down in her journals. "*A weird, jumbled catalog of all of it. The beginning of memory,*" she wrote. She chided herself for her inaction, her inability to move forward and take some sort of initiative. For Dana, the days never ended. She was never fully awake or fully asleep. She felt as though she was a sleepwalker through her own life.

Dana at her thinnest. 1997.

She needed money but wasn't doing anything about it. Day after day she wrote in her journal about being bored and unhappy and not knowing whether she still wanted to be with Morgan. Day after day she talked about getting a job but never made the effort. Even the Square was a fruitless effort. She thought about working at a strip club or maybe escorting or even becoming a dominatrix. As she was always apt to do, she was looking for someone to take her up and out of her situation. A rich man. She reached out to Jay, her escorting client, again, and considered a couple of other men, men with the means to give her the life and lifestyle she always believed she was entitled to have. She said that she loved Morgan, but she felt she deserved better, a level of sophistication that he couldn't provide.

It's difficult to imagine Dana living any sort of normal life. Perhaps on the outside she seemed in control, but whatever thoughts poured from her onto the page told a completely different story. The chaos and conflict and the extreme highs and lows of her relationship with Morgan and, indeed, with all her relationships, seemed to be essential to her being. She always wanted what she couldn't have, and that want fed her.

Every once in a while, when reading her journals, I was fortunate to get a glimpse of another Dana. The Dana who was excited about how well a chocolate chip cookie bar turned out baked in a jelly roll pan ("*I may never bake another cookie again,*" she wrote excitedly), the Dana who loved needlepoint and Bach concertos, or the Dana who gathered apples and pumpkins for Halloween and decorated their apartment for Yule.

I sometimes try—in my mind—to give her an ordinary life. I place her in a tidy apartment overlooking the French Quarter. I conjure a table holding a bowl of fruit neatly arranged in a cut glass bowl or a piece of old Yellow Ware. Frances and Mark both said that Dana loved antiques, and in this sketch, I envision her and Morgan sitting at the table and talking about the day ahead, the month ahead, their future.

This version of Morgan held her hand and told her how much he loved her. There were no harsh words, no drugs, no violence. There was soft sunlight streaming through the window on this imaginary still life, and it illuminated the table, two lovers, quiet conversation, and peace.

But reality was much different. She lost most of her things move after move. Maybe she pawned them, or maybe they were broken during arguments. Little by little, she lost pieces of herself as well.

The arguments they had—and there were many—extinguished any happiness she may have felt simply enjoying the seasons or creating a great meal. Darkness enveloped everything and it never completely went away.

An entry from July 1998 summed up her life: "*Twelve years later and I still hate my life. Different guy, different set of circumstances, same emotions. Hatred.*"

Sometimes, when she was really angry with Morgan, she scrawled HATE over and over on the pages of her journal. Other times, she allowed herself to slide into a deep depression, fueled by constant smoking. She wrote that she stayed stoned to survive.

CHAPTER 21

THE GRASS IS ALWAYS GREENER

Dana always wanted something she didn't have, be it a man or a place to live, and she emphatically believed that she deserved better than the life she was living. But, honestly, no amount of money would cure her poverty, and no caring and loving man would make her feel whole. There was a certain eroticism in the dysfunction of her relationship with Morgan, and it seemed to be something she was unwilling to leave behind.

Dana's entries in November and December 1997 were exceptionally brutal and, unfortunately, were becoming the norm. Their cocaine use—magic powder, she called it—kept her awake and agitated and questioning her beliefs, her relationship, and, when she finally crashed, her will to live. There is nothing in these journals that indicates she was working a job. She insisted she was still trying to recover from her ordeal earlier in the year, and when she felt that she should do something to earn money, it was back to possibly escorting or using her magic to bring her winning lottery tickets. When Morgan won $250 playing video poker, she said her faith and prayers were rewarded by the Gods. "*I can't deny that his windfall was my sign for me—from Odin. I feel now as if I would spit in the face of his magic if I abandoned my duty and Morgan—who is OBVIOUSLY the 'he' that was promised to me,*" she wrote on November 28. When her relationship soured—as it did in early November—she made a vow to leave him by December 7 if things didn't improve. When he won the money, she felt obligated to stay, and again, when things weren't going well in December, she set another date of February 14, 1998.

By early January, she and Morgan fought again, and he hurt her wrist. She wrapped it and, looking for answers, read her cards. "*They said it's better to stay. Who do I believe?*"

On January 10, 1998, at almost midnight, Dana typed an entry in a journal specifically set aside to write an ongoing letter to her daughters. She wanted to write to them on a regular basis. It was her only entry.

> *A year ago today was the last time we saw each other and embraced. I've been silent for a year. And for all you know nothing has changed. But it has, because I've had the vision to begin this, and I intend for this work to catalog as much wisdom as I can give you. If nothing else, it will be my legacy to you.*
>
> *This has been a dark and painful year, but I have endured. I am making a conscious effort to end my grief and continue again to move forward, hoping that this will make a difference and will help you both in your understanding of the reasons why things happened the way they did. I believe in my heart that someday these writings will serve to prove that my devotion to you and my desire to be with you never ended.*

In this letter she indicated that she felt her love for her children grow since they had been apart, and insisted that not a night went by without dreams of them. "*Really,*" she said, "*they are hauntings, and I wonder if you ever dream of me.*"

Dana tried to reason away the decisions she made, writing, "*it was for the saving of my soul that I left you behind, and for the pursuit of the true love of John Morgan, which I needed to sustain me,*" and she insisted that they all had been victims of her ex-husband's "*cruelty and narrow-mindedness.*"

She ended the entry with, "*I pray one day that you will read these words, and until then, may Thor protect you.*"

A week later, Dana wrote that as far as her daughters were concerned, she was done grieving. "*I'll put effort into something for them, but no more blood. My life is not just their loss, and they don't really care at this time anyway. There are many levels of 'the children,' but I have decided* to be done with my grief. I'm too good now to be taken down or live in the shadow of that."

Alone was the key word in January's entries. "*I spend my days in a daze—a smoke fog. Me and my soma—I've got nothing to say. Perhaps a one-act play? An article? No direction? Ahhhh!!!! Feeling the horrible need to express myself to someone!*"

As January came to a close, Dana vowed to take control of her life and to do better in her relationship with Morgan. She reveled in her weight of 115 pounds, and she adored her beautiful clothes. She was resolute.

Her determination wouldn't last.

By late February, still not working and still bored and lonely, Dana was once again fighting depression and isolation. "*The days run on together. Nothing happens. Dope and despair. Why? Why do I hate everything? Don't I have what I want? Who am I and what do I do now?*" A week after this entry, she wrote that Morgan had hit her again. "*I'm still staying. I'm still quiet and reserved.*" She insisted he had been good to her despite the fights and the blood. She continued to blame herself for the fights, for failing to understand him and his needs, and for being on the receiving end of his fists.

For quite some time, Dana and Morgan had talked about moving to Tennessee. She always dreamed about having a farm and horses and space, and she had fantasized that moving north to Tennessee could be the beginning of that life. By late March that move was a reality. However, because she was still on probation, Dana had to stay behind in New Orleans until early May. On March 19, Dana wrote, "*We are to be separated by months and great distances. I feel so deeply sad. Everything is to change in just a week. They say they'll let me alone and let me go after May 2.*"

Dana's father came to visit her at the end of March. She didn't give a reason for his visit, only that she struggled with conflicting emotions over him. Perhaps he was there to help her with her legal issues, but she never wrote about it. Maybe he told Frances that he would check on their daughter without actually revealing where she was living.

When Morgan left, Dana stayed with a friend while she completed the required community service hours. Of course, as with all of her friends, she wrote terrible things in her journals about the woman she was living with while waiting for the terms of her probation to be complete. None of Dana's friends could ever live up to her expectations, and it seemed like the only reason she kept in touch with any of them was for her own benefit.

Dana announced her *"day of vengeance"* on April 13, Frances's birthday. *"Only the two of us know,"* she wrote. *"I will never forget the act which changed me. I wrestled my vengeance from her—got my due, and I'll never regret it. I finally took what was mine."*

By the end of April, Dana had gone to another friend's house to live and she was unhappy there as well. On May 1, she wrote, *"I hate most women far more than men, I guess, 'cause most women hate me."*

On Mother's Day 1998, while still staying with her second friend and waiting to hear back from the court, she wondered what her children thought of her. I believe Dana was anguished over the loss of her children, but a part of her was also relieved that she was free of the responsibility of motherhood. On many occasions she wrote about that freedom and how much it meant to her. She equated being thin and having Morgan as a partner with success. It was an "I'll show them" attitude, them being everyone from her ex-husband to her mother.

Dana was informed on May 18 that she had a travel permit to go to Tennessee and she was absolutely ecstatic. *"It will be different, better,"* she wrote about her reunion with Morgan. *"I don't believe he'll ever hit me again and I shall stay always."*

She arrived in Tennessee on May 20, but by May 23, she was again wishing for her life to end. *"I don't believe in anything. I don't care about anything. I don't even want anything anymore. I used to believe that my beauty mattered, but I don't any longer. I don't truly believe I'm in love with him anymore."* Most likely the way Dana felt had nothing to do with Morgan and everything to do with her youngest daughter's birthday on May 24. *"Her birthday, my death day,"* she wrote.

Dana apparently found a job in early June but never said what it was, and she continued to write about her dissatisfaction with her relationship. Whether the job was temporary, she never said, but it seemed that her journal entries reflected her being at home again, looking for something to do to make money. Once again, Dana was struggling with disordered eating. Morgan was working at least two jobs.

His schedule not only included 7 A.M. to 3 P.M. shifts, but also 3 P.M. to 11 P.M. shifts and overnight shifts. She was angry when he left her but disgusted with him when he was home. Five weeks after arriving in Tennessee, she called her existence futile and thought about writing to Jay, her wealthy client from Seattle. "*I guess because I want to be saved.*"

On July 10, Dana said that she scoured the paper but didn't see anything she could or would do. "*I know it must frustrate him on some level that I'm not working at something.*"

Every entry during the month of July was filled with harsh words for Morgan and self-pity. But, on July 29, Dana received a letter from the court releasing her from probation. She was finally free. "*I'm in command again, with no one scrutinizing too closely. I pray this invigorates me, begins my renewal. It truly is a joyous day.*"

But it was only a day. Not long after, Dana's entries were the same as always. Her beauty was fading. She was getting older and had no friends. She wasn't sure she wanted to be with Morgan. She hated Tennessee.

For her thirty-fifth birthday, on August 7, she and Morgan tripped and talked about the future. She was disappointed, though, that her father forgot and never called her. "*At least I know my value with him.*" He finally called her two days later.

The remainder of her entries in August were a repeat of the months before. Oddly, interspersed in these entries were mentions of recipes, of making soup and rolls, cream cheese brownies, chops, a roast and blueberry cake. On September 12, she wrote, "*With autumn coming the cooking delights begin. I look forward to the holidays.*" It was a spark of normalcy.

I was taken by her descriptions. These were also the things I liked best about autumn. The richness of the food, the changing season, the sheer joy of cooking.

But it didn't last. The next day Dana wrote, "*Screams and arguments galore.*" She said she hated him and wanted out but had no money, no job, so how could she leave and where would she go? Later in the month she mourned for a future she would never have. "*I do so hate what's become of my life. Solace in drugs. Nothing else.*"

Regardless of what she wrote, Dana always justified staying. "*Do I really want to leave him? And for what? Will I not prove I believe in nothing that way? What use is that? I have to believe in something, and if I believe in myself and my magic, then I must concede and accept that he is what my magic wrought. And then I must love and support him. For if I don't all is lost."*

In mid-October, still virulently unhappy, Dana was hopeful that a visit from her father would help her feel better about herself and her life. However, he apparently showed up early and unannounced, and whatever happened between them, it signaled a break in that relationship as well. On October 17, she stated:

> *I guess the most important development is that I no longer believe in my heart that the man is my father. Oh, he was an obnoxious, vulgar asshole. He made my skin crawl. He is not at all of pleasant company—oh, it was gross. I cannot believe that I came from that piece of shit. I no longer have any desire to see him or know him. I believe he's served his purpose and now I'm done.*

Dana continued to lament over her on-again, off-again hate for Morgan, and her desire to make art but the inability to do so. By December, she was excited to be traveling back to New Orleans at Christmas to house-sit for a friend. She was thrilled to be going, but at the last minute changed her mind. *"I'm afraid now, afraid to be alone again. Oh, to be with him again. I don't want to go. My heart screams to just get in a cab and go back. What can be done now but to go forward? I have no choice."* Dana tried once again to salvage and mend their relationship. They forgave one another.

On December 30, Dana said she was trying as hard as she could to keep things between them smooth. *"I'm not even looking ahead. It feels like it would do no good. I don't want to let go of him. I need the security. I don't really believe that he'll truly harm me again, physically, so why not hang around?"*

In early January 1999, Dana and Morgan made the decision to leave Tennessee for Las Vegas and the thought of it thrilled her. *"I feel on the verge of something good!"* she wrote the night before leaving.

They arrived on January 14, and the following day, Dana wrote, *"Well, it's over. He and I estranged. Me, alone in a dangerous place. Shall I die? I have a week at the Thunderbird Motel to decide. I don't know what I believe about anything."*

By January 26, they were both back in New Orleans, staying at a friend's house. They were still estranged, and she blamed herself for it, writing that she felt dead and angry. *"There's nothing between us—nor will there be. I have nowhere I belong. I hate him. I'm painfully tired in my soul. I have no love. It's gone. I agonize. I am an idiot without sense or direction. I'm fat. 135 pounds. I can't let him make me fat."*

The relationship continued to be strained and she started to rapidly gain weight. She was literally horrified at this lack of self-control, adding to her growing list of disappointments. Once again, as in years past, she was obsessed about her weight, calorie counting, agonizing over clothing that no longer fit, and how tomorrow's diet would be better. She was unable to manage her weight just as she was unable to manage her life.

After a month, they found an apartment, and while she was glad to be back in New Orleans—where she felt most at home—Dana's life didn't change. She was dissatisfied and lamented about her lack of creativity, lack of money, and Morgan's inability to provide her with the lifestyle she felt she deserved. More than anything, she was lonely. *"I have no friends or family. No one,"* she wrote in September.

CHAPTER 22

AN ORPHAN AGAIN

While I literally had no bond with my adoptive mother, I did feel a sense of genuine closeness to my adoptive dad. His death brought me bitterness and a raw, lingering betrayal.

In mid-October 1999, I buried my adoptive father. He died of cancer after a five-year struggle: surgery, chemotherapy, and dialysis. He was diagnosed in 1994. I got the call one afternoon while my husband and I were restoring the front porch of our house. The doctor gave my dad two years, at most, but he was determined to beat those odds. I offered up a silent prayer, to a god I didn't really believe existed, that I would give up five years of my life so he could have five more added to his.

A family member often drove him to dialysis during the last year of his life, and it was during these weekly trips that my father confided in him about the dire state of his finances. His son was to blame. Their only biological child, he had been treated like royalty and given anything he wanted as a child. They bought him a car, paid for his college, and helped in ways I would never know. Now in his mid-thirties, divorced and with a girlfriend in Canada, he needed money to maintain a lavish lifestyle for her and her children. He bought her a car and a house, and set up trusts for her children. All of the money for this came from my parents.

It had reached a point where he would write out checks when he wanted or needed cash, and eventually he drained nearly all of their savings and investments. I learned about what was happening late in the game, and for whatever reason, neither of my parents felt as though they should tell me anything. My mother always defended her son, regardless of what he'd done. This was her miracle baby, her only real child. She would protect him to the end. It was me who was the outsider in all of this.

When my father's health declined to the point he could no longer be cared for at home—it was the late summer of that year—he was placed in a nursing facility. He was so angry and hurt by this, that his family would abandon him in this way, that he stopped talking. Despite my regular visits to see him, he refused to speak a word. I remember two occasions in particular. One was a warm and sunny autumn day, a rare, picture-perfect afternoon. I wheeled him outside because I thought he would enjoy the fresh air and the changing leaves. He simply sat there, absolutely motionless and completely silent. My mother came with me, and, despite his deteriorating state, she smiled the vacant smile I would come to know as her way of expressing denial and disbelief. She talked to him as though nothing was wrong. Even at the end of his life, she was fully expecting him to get out of that chair, get dressed, and leave.

The second was an evening event at the nursing home, a formal dance that I could only describe as a cotillion of the absurd. That night was more Kafkaesque than real to me as I watched the residents dressed in gowns and suits—no doubt sourced by the staff from various thrift shops—crowding the room, more than a few oblivious to the Big Band music that provided the evening's soundtrack. My father, wearing a baggy sweater and slumped in his wheelchair, sat in a corner and didn't even bother to look up. At that point I felt that I was killing him by keeping him there, and I would have done just about anything to take him home.

It was awful to witness his decline. He was a hard worker all his life, and even with mounting health issues, he refused to stop working. Seeing him this way, barely able to be transferred from a bed to a wheelchair, was agonizing.

The night he died, I was with him until well after midnight. His voice was barely a whisper, and it was a struggle for him to talk. He did manage to make a few quips about football and whether the Steelers would have a good season, and that made me smile. His next words were far from funny. On the night he died, my adoptive dad told me, "I raised the devil." Those were the last words he spoke to me, and they were directed toward his son. His son, though, wasn't with him that night because he was in jail, arrested for stealing from his current employer.

I still remember the drive home: the deserted road, the leaves scattered on the pavement in front of me, the surreal feeling that my father's life was at its end. Only minutes after I walked through my front door, a nurse called and said he had taken a turn for the worse. By the time I reached the hospital, my adoptive father had died. Although I've often heard it said that we all die alone, his last moments should have been better. He should have had someone with him. I felt guilty for that, that my father had no one to hold his hand during the finality of his life and no one to help him remember the good things about his seventy-seven years. And for me, there were plenty of good memories of my dad. But they were mostly crowded in the space of years before his son entered adolescence.

My dad and I fished together, and I still remember the day I caught my first fish at age six. He put me on top of a large rock along the shore of a small stream called Medix Run, and told me to fish there and not leave that spot. I had a small creel strapped across my shoulder, and in it was a green metal container filled with worms we'd dug out of the garden that morning. I was so excited to have a fish on the end of my line that I yelled, "I caught one! I caught one!" I'm sure the other fishermen along the stream were thrilled.

We hunted together, too. When I was thirteen he bought me a .410 shotgun for my birthday to hunt small game, and I used an ancient octagon barrel 30-30 rifle for deer. My favorite days were when we went squirrel hunting. We'd walk up into the woods after I got home from school, beyond where the old '42 mine had been and near to our deer stands, and sit ourselves on the side hill among the maple and oak leaves. It didn't matter to me whether we saw anything or not. It was a splendid time of year, my favorite, and mostly we didn't even talk. It was just good being out there with him.

In late summer 1973, when I was nearly thirteen, he took me with him on a search for men he worked with in the mines in the 1940s and '50s. He needed their signed affidavits as part of the documentation necessary to file a claim with the U.S. Department of Labor. Preliminary tests showed that he had a condition called pneumoconioses, a group of lung diseases caused by the lung's reaction to inhaling certain dusts. The main cause is workplace exposure. In my father's case, his was caused by working in coal mines. He had Black Lung.

He began working in the mines in the early 1940s, and in 1943, he received a Bituminous Miner's Certificate of Competency and Qualification from the Commonwealth of Pennsylvania Department of Mines. At the time, he was employed by the Shawmut Mining Company, one of the area's largest mining firms. After serving in the army during World War II, he returned home and went back to the mines until the mid-1950s. In total, he worked at seven different mines in three counties during those years, and part of his claim had to contain proof of that employment.

My memory of those trips is fuzzy at best, but I was his sidekick during the summer of 1973, riding beside him in his big brown Plymouth. He initially filed a claim in 1979, and it was denied in 1980. He eventually hired a local attorney to handle the case and to navigate the appeals process. His benefits claim was again denied in 1987, and once more the decision was appealed. He kept all the letters, court decisions, and medical test results in a large tan envelope. His benefit claim was finally awarded in April 1990, and his benefit award was made retroactive to his initial filing in 1979. His owed benefits totaled over $70,000, and his monthly check moving forward was $557. I remember when that letter arrived. He was absolutely ecstatic. After nearly a dozen years, mountains of paperwork and tests, and two appeals, the courts agreed that he did indeed qualify for Black Lung benefits. It was ironic, celebrating a monthly check for something that would likely kill him. I helped him fill out some of the later paperwork, and one of the documents included information on his dependents. His son was listed as a student and legitimate. I was listed as adopted.

~∞∞~

When I returned to the hospital that night, his room was dark, save for one soft light that was lit above the headboard of the bed. He was covered with a sheet to his neck. Gone was the man with the dry wit, with the amazing garden, with the patience for woodworking and hunting and an immense love for baseball. His life didn't end like he imagined, I'm sure, and I think that he died as much from a broken heart as anything cancer threw at him.

In helping my adoptive mom with funeral arrangements and other necessary paperwork, I came across an insurance policy they had purchased for my daughter when she was a baby.

I wasn't even the beneficiary; that honor was given to their son. I was absolutely stunned. It was the proverbial icing on the cake and it summed up what I felt I actually meant to them. Their son would benefit if anything horrible would have happened to my daughter. I also came across my father's recently amended will. Apparently during the final year of his life, my adoptive father had a change of heart. His son was completely excluded.

My adoptive mom would live nearly eleven years longer than my dad, and her son continued to squeeze what little money was left. I was her Power of Attorney, and her checking account required my signature to cash any checks, but it didn't stop him from having her sign $175,000 of savings bonds—which I didn't know even existed—and cash them all. When I discussed this with the bank manager, he insisted that she signed them and there was nothing he could do about it. When I pushed back, he brushed me off and told me to sue them. When there was really nothing remaining in her accounts but a few thousand dollars, both my adoptive mother and brother showed up at my workplace, distraught, begging me to please give them money. I refused. It was the last time I saw him.

My mother, eventually unable to take care of herself, spent time in assisted living and then a nursing home. During all those years, nearly a decade, her son never once visited her. She asked for him; she insisted that one of the contractors working on the HVAC system in the nursing home was him. She believed he would show up any day.

They are all together now, mother, father, and son.

He died in September 2021 at age fifty-six.

I wasn't listed in his obituary.

CHAPTER 23

NO SUCH THING AS ENOUGH

Dana's drug of choice was pot. There are literally hundreds of mentions of it in her journals, and she hated being without it. It was cocaine, though, that took Dana and Morgan to the very bottom, to less than zero.

Back in New Orleans there were plenty of drugs, and by mid-1999, they took their place front and center in Dana and Morgan's relationship. At first it was flirtatious. She felt *"wild and free"* when she did cocaine. Life was an endless party. Life was drugs. And she believed that she and Morgan were closer because of them.

She wrote:

> *Coke and drinks for breakfast. No sleep*
> *Coke, wine, and smoke. Aren't we having fun?*
> *Ecstasy and acid.*

But there was a tipping point, and beyond that it wasn't fun, it wasn't recreation, it wasn't a way to expand her mind. It was survival. *"I pray for more drugs,"* she wrote. *"I just want all the edges blurred."*

She wanted independence, freedom, money. But much of what was earned was spent on drugs. It would continue to get worse and worse up until some of the final words she wrote in August 2001. She said that she and Morgan were *"built on drugs. What are we without them?"*

In late October, Dana said that doing ecstasy with him made them close. Five days later she wrote that he choked her again.

That autumn was filled with nightmares about her children and the loss of them in her life. She bemoaned the lack of any friends and family. She again started writing about her weight, her lack of self-control, and how old and ugly she felt. In November she called her relationship broken again and wrote that Morgan spit on her.

A few days before Thanksgiving, Dana wrote in her journal by candlelight while she planned a menu for the holiday and made a list of what she needed. "*The trimmings and feasting make the season for me,*" she said, and she was thrilled to wear new jeans, boots, and a cashmere sweater. "*I'll feel luxuriant!*" But, as always, a fight with Morgan ruined everything. As the weeks went on, things got no better.

She divulged that Morgan threatened her with a gun, pushed her, cursed her, and "*told me he should just shoot me,*" and still, at the end of the year, she said she continued to love him and hoped for a bright future in 2000.

She decorated the apartment for Yule and was joyous over the beginning of winter. By Christmas Eve, it had all come crashing down. On Christmas Day, 1999, she wrote, "*Well, here we are. Gun parts on the floor. My kids are opening their presents or already have. And here I am, alone, in myself. Is it him or the security I need?*"

Another holiday, another huge fight. But by New Year's Day, she was in love with him again and hoped that 2000 would be her year.

Were things finally going her way? She was thrilled by the possibility of singing with a band. It made her genuinely happy. These bright spots were fewer and fewer as time went on. Dana was stood up by at least one other band during her time in New Orleans, but this project seemed like a sure thing. She was ecstatic.

She wrote:

> *Me at 36 finally to sing on Bourbon Street and get paid. Gods! Dare I dream of this? . . . I would rehearse as much as I could. I would have achieved a success that I dreamed of so deeply for so long. To belong to a band! To have mates again! And the music—to let it all pour out of me. It's been so long since I've done anything I'm proud of.*

This blues band, some of its members from Norway, seemed like an answer to a lifelong dream. "*I drift off to sleep in the satisfaction of knowing that they were <u>all</u> wrong about me.*"

By early March she said that rehearsals were good and she was feeling hopeful. By mid-March it all fell apart. *"Why did it have to turn out wrong again?"* she moaned.

Reading her words, no matter how many times, broke my heart, because there seemed to be so few things in her life that brought her actual joy. In one of her entries, she mentioned a tape she had singing with this band. That, like so much of her life, was most likely thrown out with the trash. Mark said she had a wonderful singing voice. It saddens me that I will never hear it.

By the spring of 2000, Dana's entries reflected a world that seemed to diminish as the months passed, becoming smaller, darker, dirtier, and meaner. Every candle that burned in her life was extinguished, one by one, until it was impossible to find her way.

They fought again. She cried again. She admitted that she hadn't wanted a life with Morgan ever since May 1997, when he hit her. And yet she didn't have the *"energy or desire"* to leave. He was the devil she knew, and she believed no one else would want her.

"I am a wasted, useless, drug addicted whore."

Maybe, she hoped, life could begin when she lost twenty pounds. Then she could leave him.

She set goals. Those goals were never met. The bar for happiness was so low that she was relieved when they didn't fight for twenty-two days.

Little by little she lost what tiny piece of joy that remained in her life. There would be no fame, no career, no recognition. *"I am no one grand. I am a crazy idiot and always have been,"* she wrote in June 2000.

The focus of daily life was cocaine. And she didn't care that all their money went to buy coke.

"Three more bags. Clarity. Not caring about the physical consequences."
"More coke. No dinner. I don't care. I love the rebellion."

By early August, she thought that perhaps she should stop partying so much, but on her thirty-seventh birthday, her gift was *"all the coke I could want."* More cocaine. More arguments. More threats to kill her.

On September 1, they moved again, to 735 Ursulines Avenue.

This would be her final move.

While she loved to be alone, she hated the loneliness of that place. She would mark time by Morgan's coming and going, smoke a bowl or two, and try again—like so many other periods in her life—to write a story or a book or a play. *"To capture a feeling, a moment with words. I think that is my greatest talent."* Until she gave up. There were very few dreams left at 735 Ursulines Avenue.

She mourned the loss of her children, and she wondered if they even remembered her. She felt that she deserved better, that all her life she had never been truly loved. In November, she even thought that perhaps she shouldn't have left her husband. *"The children are gone. It's all gone. With nothing left but pain and remorse."*

A small piece of happiness was her dog, Ginger, a Yorkie, whom she seemed to love most of the time. This was a pattern with her. She would get a pet, it would do something to annoy her or make her mad, and she would get rid of it. Over the years she had a bird, a rabbit, cats, and dogs. Always their fate was the same.

One time, Mark remembered, Dana believed that a kitten she had adopted had infected her daughters with ringworm. She told the woman who gave her the cat that she wanted to give it back. When she refused, Dana put it in the woman's mailbox on a hot summer day in Florida. Dana, too, could be extremely cruel.

Dana had always believed she had special powers, insight, magic. But by late 2000, she wrote that she was nothing. *"No goddess. No witch. I have no unusual power or ability. I'm merely insane. I have been all my life."*

She and Morgan fought, and when she hit him during one of their arguments, he threatened her again with a gun.

"I, too, am unhappy like my mother was," she declared. *"I did not manage to escape the curse of stupid choices."* She reflected on her twenty-two years of journal-keeping. *"I've always lived mostly in my mind,"* she wrote. *"Reading has been my escape. Still is."*

She leaned on her journal heavily, more so than at any other time of her life, and she truly believed it was her closest friend. *"I don't know how you've come to have a sentience, but I feel you listen."* At the end of the year, she prophesied that she doubted she would live to see forty. *"But who cares anyway?"*

As usual, another holiday was ruined by fighting, and on Christmas Eve, she hoped that her children slept well and were well. *"I miss you. Four years. I never knew you. Will I ever?"* On Christmas Day, still far from a place of redemption, she wrote that she hated her parents and she hoped they were suffering. *"I hope you are dying or dead. Escaping you, all of you, is deliciously sweet still.*

CHAPTER 24

HATRED AND HEARTACHE

*I look for the teenage Dana in her final words, and I wonder what happened to
the young woman who dreamed such big dreams. I will never understand why she
refused to leave Morgan, knowing that after years of dissatisfaction and abuse,
there was no grand oath for her to abide, no gods commanding she stay with this
man. Had she so little self-worth that she believed this was all she deserved?*

Of all of Dana's journals, the final one, beginning on June 5, 2001,
through August 30, 2001, was the most comprehensive. Many of the
entries were typed and pasted on the pages. As her life unraveled, she
chronicled it all in obsessive detail.

> *I stare at these words, the only true comfort I have, and I think, how
> long will I sit alone writing letters to myself? How long will I let
> this go on? And I think that when I am finally better and can walk
> around again and can get a job, well then I can begin planning. Right
> now, my job is to keep calm and quiet and not reveal the true nature
> of my feelings. I find that I censor myself even here, out of fear that
> you will be read and I will be held accountable for what I've written,
> even though this is the only place I feel safe to talk about how I feel.*

In early June, Dana was recovering from a broken foot so she was
unable to work. Injury aside, she dreaded going back to her job at the
deli where they were both employed, the Quartermaster.

"It doesn't matter that I doubt and mistrust, or that I've felt abused. I still stay. I can't leave. Who knows why? Must be love?" she wrote on the first page of this final journal. She promised that she would stop using the "H word" (hate) in reference to Morgan, and she vowed to protect him with *"better magic in the future."*

The last eight months of journal entries were painfully similar and difficult to read, and this one was by far the most gut-wrenching. Dana wrote that she believed her life was over, *"and all I'm doing is waiting to die."*

Every day was the same. Morgan's cocaine addiction was out of control. Dana began hiding cash and guns all over the apartment. She couldn't trust Morgan to pay the bills, nor could she trust that he wouldn't shoot her. She was sure he was hiding coke in the house and, despite him telling her otherwise, she knew he was using, and that he had never stopped.

She had no faith in his ability to take care of her, and she was disillusioned by the choices she'd made in her life. She was emotionally drained and tired of having to deal with Morgan's problems. *"He can't keep his shit together for more than two days in a row. He truly is worse than I am, and I didn't think that was possible."*

Despite this, there was something about him that she still wanted and she gave him until October 31 to turn himself around and be a better partner. *"All I can do is give it until I hit 130 pounds and the autumn comes. Then reassess. No trust. He doesn't deserve it. How not to hate?"*

Over and over, she described how sad and lonely she was and how she was fed up with his behavior and his addiction. She contemplated *"quietly and carefully"* creating a support system so she could escape.

Her children were on her mind. *"I miss my children. I wish I knew them. But I cannot touch it for eight more years. 2009. Then I'll be 46 . . . 20 years ago—high school graduation."*

Those early journals were written when life was full of such promise. Now, in this final journal, it was all Dana could do to get through the day. *"All you are is pain to me,"* she said of Morgan. *"Our lives will never change."* She vowed to find a loving, kind, and caring man, one that would *"provide for me, protect me, devote himself to me above all."* All the things that Dana said about Morgan when she first met him.

Any semblance of a normal relationship was long gone. Over and over, she detailed her constant anger and hatred of him. *"No days without* tears, strife, ugliness. *My life is a catalog of pain.*" She was afraid of him. She never doubted that he could and would hurt her if he so chose, and she wondered whether he had killed someone before: "*I have no proof of anything, other than once I saw the name Morgan on his military uniform pictures. I never met the elusive sister.*"

Was it a genuine fear of him that kept her in the relationship or a fear of being alone? "*I continue to examine myself and I'm trying to figure a way out of this situation safely, and I don't see one. He won't ever willingly let me go without a fight . . . He'll threaten me, even if he starts out acting like he's going to be reasonable. I fear him. I can only carefully plan and keep my mouth shut.*"

On June 19, not long after midnight, Dana revealed that he locked her in the apartment. In an entry typed at 1:39 A.M., she said:

> *I couldn't stand it. I called the store and there was an answering machine. No way to get through, and so I kept calling and then he called back, and I screamed bloody murder at him for locking me in again. He says it was to keep me safe, and I said he cannot do that again. I hate him with everything inside me . . . I am unhappy as I have ever been in my life.*

Morgan locked her in the apartment at least twice, and she admitted, "*he has done things to me that I thought I would never tolerate from anyone. And I am embarrassed that I am still here taking it.*" She called him a pot ready to boil over because life "*is not the way he wants it,*" and she blamed herself for the life she was now living. "*I could have done different things, but I chose sex and drugs and stimuli to get away from the past I hated. And now I hate this.*"

He made her feel inadequate, and she knew there would be no happy ending, but she wrote that she didn't know how to live without him.

> *I was thinking before I went to sleep that my chances of leaving him, despite me railing and ranting here, are fairly slim. I barely trust him after seven years. Who else could I trust? I have fixed ideas about myself that are not going to go away, and no other man would tolerate me. Really, they would all just dump me. I'm nearly 40.*

Her entries were dark. It was always about escape but with no means to do it. She admitted that in real life, she pretends that everything is going to be okay *"WHEN I KNOW INSIDE MYSELF THAT IT IS NOT GOING TO BE OK!"*

Regardless of how nice Morgan treated her from time to time, there was always an undercurrent of violence, and she never did feel completely safe. She wrote that she felt fat and ugly and *"as if my life is at an end."*

She and Morgan had apparently talked about eventually leaving New Orleans and traveling to North Dakota. There was no particular reason to pick that place, but Dana was dreaming again about a farm and horses and working the land and that somehow someone would give them a loan to buy a ranch. One day she insisted that she was ready to leave New Orleans because it had changed so much. A few days later she railed about Morgan and how she would never, ever leave her home there and go anywhere with him.

Because her plan was to save as much money as possible, she had no choice but to go back to work. At the end of June, she made a decision to go back to the Quartermaster on July 13. She tried to remember all the things she liked about the deli. She was a manager, didn't have to work alone, and enjoyed seeing the cops who stopped by for a meal, playing the Heart song "Even it Up" on the jukebox, and being close to Morgan. She talked herself into taking the job again.

And yet, she still wrote about trying to escape, of marrying almost anyone who would offer her security. She was even considering asking her friend Darryl, who was gay. She would do almost anything to leave her situation.

On July 19, she explained what had transpired over the past few days:

> *Gods, where do I begin? 24 hours ago we were in the midst of another fight, which lasted until 9 A.M. When I forgave him of taking $140 more and spending it on Tuesday night. He was high as a kite all night at work, and they gave him two triple bags in addition to all that he bought. He was high all day yesterday. And there's one triple left that I bought him on Tuesday. The whole thing is driving me crazy . . . I have no idea how to handle him anymore.*

One day later, on his birthday, she sent him out with her last forty dollars for his final birthday *"amusement."* And then Dana wrote this:

> *I am only doing myself a disservice by living a lie, and I'm lying to myself as well. I am crazy for this man. That's why my emotions are so extreme. And I've let my heart become divided, and now I'm fighting with myself only, because I keep reconciling with him. I allowed him to slide with adultery. How can I not, I can't keep my hands off of him. And when the pendulum swings over to hate, I seem to love more violently afterwards. Seven years ago I spent his birthday with him on five hits of acid. Something began then. It hasn't ended. And I don't want it to. I want it to be him, always. I guess I don't really care what becomes of us. As long as we are together.*

Up until the end of August 2001, she refused to leave him. She wrote of it constantly, of escaping, but in the end, she was more afraid of being alone. She was more afraid of the future without him than what he was capable of doing to her.

On August 30, Dana confessed that Morgan *"stole my money, lied about the rent, stole for drugs, beat me. Part of me hates him with a burning hatred, and the other part has lust and desire for him to save me and heal my life. It's a miserable, weird relationship that most of the time I wish were different."*

But she didn't lose sight of the fact that someday he would have to account for his actions. *"Oh let's just write it: I hate you and the pain you've caused me. I won't forget it. Ever. Someday you'll pay for what you've done to me, one way or the other."*

The year 2001 was the first time since 1996 that Dana didn't pen an entry on April 13 cursing Frances, and she admitted that her life had *"become a nightmare that was predicted, and my mother was right. This man is not worth what my children would have meant to me. I was a fool, and I'll die alone as a fool."*

And, as she had done each year, she marked the birthdays of her daughters, regretting the path she had chosen. It made her feel old that her children were now ten and twelve, and she was gone from them longer than she was with them.

A day before her own birthday, Dana wrote, *"Why do birthdays always feel so exciting? Perhaps it's because it belongs to me alone."* There were no flowers or cards or gifts from Morgan that year. He was preoccupied with finding more cocaine. A week later, she said that she was still stung by the ruin of the day, but penned this, addressing the entry directly to her journal: *"It sure is pleasant to have you to talk to. There is no one else."*

Despite all this unhappiness, Dana kept convincing herself that somehow it would get better, that he would change, that he would love her as she felt she deserved to be loved. Her entries were the writings of a woman who knew that she had to leave for her own good but somehow couldn't do it. Not until she saved $3,000, not until after Halloween, not until she lost thirty pounds. *"Because if I must leave him, I must also be ready to find another man."*

CHAPTER 25

I'M DEATH, I COME TO TAKE THE SOUL, LEAVE THE BODY AND LEAVE IT COLD

I still remember reading the article in the Times-Picayune about the mummified corpse found stuffed in a cheap foot locker during the Katrina cleanup. I looked for any information I could find about the discovery after Frances told me that she had been contacted by the police in New Orleans for information about Dana. I emailed the link to my brother, Mark, and watched helplessly as my mother's life unraveled. After my initial reading of Dana's journals, these were the first words I wrote:

False god

He told her he was a god
and she believed him.
Through evictions,
black eyes,
broken bones
and cocaine-fueled arguments,
she believed him.
Until he wrapped the cord around her neck
so tight
she couldn't breathe.

Until
finally,
in her last gasp for breath
she knew he had lied.

~~~~∞∞~~~~

The *Times-Picayune*
November 3, 2005

A body found last month sticking out of a footlocker on the North Rampart Street neutral ground is believed to be a homicide victim of months or even years ago, police said Wednesday.

A person walking past Elysian Fields Avenue and North Rampart Street flagged down a soldier on Oct. 21 after noticing a body sticking out of a footlocker in some hurricane debris, police said.

The body was not a Katrina victim, police spokesman Capt. Marlon Defillo said. It was in a state of advanced decomposition—in fact, "It was close to skeletal remains," Defillo said. The coroner's office classified the death as a homicide, Defillo said, but authorities wouldn't say how that determination was reached, or discuss the cause of death.

"We are hesitant to release the exact cause of death because at this point it may compromise the investigation," Defilio said.

At least two officers said police believe the victim was a New Orleans woman and that homicide Detective Gregory Hamilton has been taking her background . . .

It would be revealed at Morgan's trial that it was actually the landlord of his apartment, and not a passerby, who opened the trunk after dragging it out of the apartment building and forcing open the lock.

My sister always dreamed of fame and fortune. She grieved over never being noticed, and in every journal, there are at least a few entries about being denied the celebrity she felt she deserved. It is a twisted irony that this notoriety should come to her long after her death.

For me, it is strange how the anniversary of Katrina makes me feel. There is a longing for something I will never have. A loss of a piece of me. Dana had already been dead for three years when Katrina ravaged the city, but if not for Katrina, Dana's body may never have been found.

CHAPTER 26

30 X 16.5 X 15.5

My Pretty Polly, not even given the honor of a good death. For as many times as Dana wished to die, I doubt she would have wished for this. This man, who she once worshipped as some sort of god, hacked her to pieces and threw her away like a used-up carcass. The details were revealed at Dana's murder trial and again at a Court of Appeals hearing in December 2010.

Inside the trunk that contained the body—a trunk that measured 30 x 16.5 x 15.5 inches—police found a pair of socks, a curling iron electrical cord that was tangled inside the body, a white sheet, a white towel, a pair of underwear, sweatpants, a beer can, mothballs, an Ace bandage, and a small American flag. The arms and legs had been cut from the torso. The body was in an advanced state of decomposition. From the chest up, including the head, the body was skeletonized. There were only a few pieces of tissue remaining. The extremities were also skeletonized, with a few pieces of muscle and dried skin remaining. The tissue that remained on the torso and hip region was mummified.

~⚭~

Morgan and his new girlfriend had been living in the Elysian Fields Avenue apartment where the trunk had been stored. Morgan told the owner of the apartment that he didn't want any of his belongings that were in the storage room of the apartment.

The photo was taken when the trunk containing Dana's remains was found on North Rampart Street in October 2005

While clearing the property of storm debris, the landlord dragged the trunk outside. He forced open the lock and dumped out its contents. Inside the trunk was a decomposed mummified body.

In Morgan's apartment, in a small lockbox, the landlord's companion found Dana's driver's license, passport, birth certificate, Sears credit card, social security card, a Ramada Inn check stub, Chattanooga library card, Seventh Avenue customer card, and an Adult Probation Department letter. Also in the box were a number of items belonging to Morgan, including a subpoena to appear in Criminal District Court on March 8, 2002.

Frances was contacted by the New Orleans police and told of the discovery in the autumn of 2005. Initially, a tibia bone from the body was sent to the FBI crime lab for DNA analysis. Later, because the bone was too dry to test, a tooth was sent for testing. An FBI agent reached out to Frances, obtained a DNA sample, and forwarded it to the crime lab for mitochondrial DNA comparison to the tooth taken from the body. Frances waited and worried, hoping beyond hope that the corpse belonged to someone else.

In July 2007, the FBI confirmed that the body was positively identified as Dana's.

Mark said that Frances had the crime scene photos, and she would often look at them and try to convince herself that what was left of the woman in that foot locker was not her daughter.

John Henry Morgan, born John Alan Roberson, was arrested on February 8, 2008, in North Carolina. In June 2008, he was formally charged with one count of second-degree murder.

When Morgan was interviewed by the police following his arrest in 2008, he admitted that he had a bad drug habit while living in New Orleans. He said he used cocaine, marijuana, acid, and mushrooms, and told police that most of his money went to support that habit. In that interview, he also admitted to keeping Dana's body, but he denied killing her. He also said he never thought of calling the police.

The videotaped interview he gave police was, at one time, online. It was chilling because he was so calm in his explanation of how he dismembered Dana so he could fit her into the trunk.

Following a three-day jury trial on July 27–29, 2009, in New Orleans, he was found guilty as charged. At the trial, Assistant District Attorney Francesca Bridges told jurors that "she was a thing he had in his apartment that was decomposing. A thing that he was trying to forget was his girlfriend."

In August 2009, he was sentenced to life imprisonment at hard labor without the benefit of parole. He unsuccessfully appealed his conviction in 2010.

Morgan sits in a cell in prison, and Dana's ashes are in an urn at my brother's house.

CHAPTER 27

THE MISSING PIECE

My sister considered her journals an extension of herself. She took care of them and she made certain that they were safe and, toward the end of her life, found solace within their pages. It makes absolutely no sense to me that she would abruptly stop writing. If nothing else, Dana would have written even more because she had no one else to talk to.

I often think of those last months and I believe there must have been at least one more journal, spanning from September 2001 to March 2002. It would have been completely out of character for Dana to stop writing.

Maybe Morgan found it and destroyed it.

Maybe someone in New Orleans still has it.

I believe Dana had always hoped someone would eventually read her journals, which is why she made certain they were kept safe. Did she have a premonition of her own death? Did she entrust them to a friend because of that? Even with her life so out of control, she had enough foresight to give someone the journals, who could assure her that they would survive. So they, as she once said, would be her legacy.

Perhaps I want to know that there is another journal, that it exists somewhere out there, and that in those pages, Dana had an epiphany and decided to move back to Ohio and pull her life together. That she wanted to see her mother again, reunite with her children, hold out an olive branch to her brother. I want to believe that she had finally had enough: She was really going to walk out that door and leave.

More than anything, I need to believe that she wanted to live.

It was interesting to me how, during testimony at the trial, their coworkers claimed that Dana and Morgan had a cordial and professional relationship while both were employed at the Quartermaster Deli. She apparently confided in no one regarding the state of her personal life.

The journal that quickly became her confidante when she was a teenager was the only thing she trusted with her feelings. It was her beginning and her end, and the time she spent writing seemed to Dana to be the only real moments in her life.

Most of the final journal entries are focused on how much money Morgan was spending on cocaine. On July 17, 2001, she wrote that she gave him $100 to buy coke so he would come home.

On August 30, 2001, in her final entry in the last journal, she wrote: "*I am no longer depressed. Nor do I want my life to end. I want to make some of it yet. I want to see my children again. In the next few months I want to begin singing again. I am determined to LIVE here. Somehow I promise myself, I will succeed at something and be happy. I will.*"

She said these sorts of things many times over the course of her nearly eight-year relationship with Morgan, but did she finally mean them this time? Her will to leave had always been fleeting, but was this time different? I would like to think so, but in all likelihood, the next entry may have been all about forgiving him and keeping her oath to stay together.

I wonder about Dana's last day. What did she say that made Morgan so angry that he did finally take her life? It could have been anything, really. They fought over mundane things. In one instance she wrote about a row they had over take-out food.

Was he high? Did he need more cocaine and did she refuse to give him money? Did she berate him, belittle him, and call him out for being useless to her? Morgan strangled her with the cord of her curling iron. Was she getting ready for work, standing in front of the mirror in the bathroom? Was it an argument that escalated further than any prior confrontation, or did he simply snap after Dana said something caustic?

Strangulation is the ultimate form of power and control, and perhaps Morgan, once and for all, showed her who was really in charge. Strangulation is also considered one of the most lethal forms of domestic violence, and given their abusive relationship, that it escalated to this isn't surprising.

Dana must have been terrified, and the pain must have been excruciating. Did she violently fight back as she struggled to breathe? As she lapsed into unconsciousness, did she relive her life and finally realize that from the first time she allowed him to abuse her that this was her destiny?

Brain death from strangulation takes only five minutes, and as she slumped to the floor, did Morgan step back and truly understand that Dana was dead? Did this realization send him into a panic or provide him with a sense of relief? There she was, a 150-pound woman, dead on the floor of their apartment. What do you do with a dead body when you don't have a vehicle? Where do you put it? How do you keep it a secret? Most importantly, perhaps, how do you clean up the mess?

Morgan's former landlord, Maria Barranco, testified at his trial that she asked him what had happened to Dana, and he allegedly told her Dana had been in an accident. Barranco said she smelled an odor coming from the trunk but testified that Morgan said it was from a dead rat. "It was disgusting; it smelled terrible and you can still smell that stuff in my apartment," the *Times-Picayune* reported Barranco saying. "How could you live with something like that?"

And what do you do with your life afterward? Morgan made up plenty of stories to explain Dana's disappearance.

Dana enjoyed talking to the police officers who ate at the deli while writing their reports. Detective Aaron Crunk testified at Morgan's trial that one evening, Dana told him and the other officers that she was leaving the city and moving back to her hometown. He never saw her again.

A week later, he asked Morgan about Dana, and Morgan told him that she had been involved in a car accident and was in the hospital. Detective Crunk told the court that he asked Morgan for the name and address of the hospital so he could send her a card. Morgan never responded and quit working at the deli. Detective Crunk said that he saw Morgan briefly afterward and described him as very skinny, "sickly looking," and aloof. How sad that this police officer thought enough of Dana to ask about her and want to send her a card. Dana, on the other hand, thought no one noticed her, no one cared about her. She only had to look across the counter at one of her customers.

The magic community had a lot to say online about Morgan and the murder. One of the group said he always thought that Morgan was rather devoid of emotion. "*Hard to even know what was going on with him, even while tripping with him,*" he wrote in his blog. "*I like to think that if I trip with people I kinda know them . . . I like to think the know the people fairly well. I guess I have been wrong on that one!*"

Another individual posting to this site wrote that, long before Dana left, there was speculation about Morgan being abusive to his partners:

> *As for the motivations of keeping the body around . . . only John knows the answer to that. Could be control, warped affection, fear, some magical belief system or something else. John was not stable, more than one person had problems with him, he set off warning buzzers and lights in most women.*

Dana's final resting place was a cheap tan and gray particleboard trunk, one that he kept in his possession for years. After a while—her remains were mummified by the time the trunk was pried open after it was set out for the trash months following Katrina—he could have easily bagged her body one piece at a time and put it out to the curb with the rest of his garbage. No one would have known. But maybe he liked this Dana better; he could finally control her. So he kept her around.

Tucked in the pages of one of her journals is a letter from Morgan to Dana, written in beautiful, flowing script. It is undated.

> *For my dear sweet Polly,*
> *May inspiration flow from your pen, and may you always feel my love for you like a shield protecting you from the ills of the world.*
> *I love you,*
> *John Morgan*

CHAPTER 28

WHO AM I, REALLY?

Throughout my life, I never had a name for what I felt, but the effects of separation and abandonment, and the inability to form close relationships, was always there. Books like The Primal Wound *gave credence to what I was experiencing.*

Life is a series of losses. My first loss was my mother.

When I envision a woman carrying her child for nine months, talking to that child, singing to it, nurturing it, the thought of giving that infant—that part of her—away to someone else is beyond heartbreaking. There is loss. It is as though that child died. Because, for the birth mother, that is certainly the case. While she can hope, that young woman—the "once mother"—has to know that chances are this child is dead to her.

And even, *even* if they find one another later in life, there is no way to put it all back together again. There is only loss; the adoptee will never belong to either world. We search for something that is impossible to mend.

At times I feel as though I need to ask permission to speak of Dana, as though I don't have the right to claim her as my sister. At times I feel I don't belong to anyone.

My relationship with my birth mom changed after everyone finally knew, through DNA testing, that the corpse in the trunk was Dana. She distanced herself from me. The dead daughter was better. Of course, I could have done more to hold up my end of the relationship. Frances wanted me to come with her to New Orleans for the trial, and I was unable to do so. That seemed to be the tipping point for our relationship. She eventually shut me out. She wouldn't answer my calls. During one of our final conversations, she told me that I was hard to love.

Frances was driven deep into a black place of mourning, and she had no intention of ever coming back. To me, she willfully wished for death, and she wanted that death to be in the farmhouse in Ohio where Dana grew up because she felt that Dana was still there with her. That wouldn't happen. She died on December 26, 2019, in a long-term nursing facility, and she called out Dana's name right before she took her final breath.

Mark said it grieves him that our mother, who was such a warrior in so many ways, died such an unceremonious death.

~~~⁂~~~

As I read Dana's words, I can envision her as a person, alive and beautiful. My blood.

I always think of her on her birthday and equate it with the beginning of the harvest season, with ripe tomatoes and squash and beans, warm nights, overflowing pots of bright geraniums. She comes to mind when I scour a cookbook for a dessert recipe—smiling at her journal entries about getting those brownies just right—or when I make a kettle of butternut squash soup in the first crisp days of autumn. I will always remember Frances telling me what a great cook Dana was, and that she had a knack for developing recipes.

I wonder, if she *was* able to see the future, would she still have stayed in that broken life with a man she mostly hated? Would anything have changed her mind?

Maybe I feel sorry for myself or have some sort of fucked up survivor's guilt. The daughter who was given away lives, while the daughter who was my birth mom's love child dies. I've always stood in the shadow of their lives; a presence, but not a wholly physical being. Legally, I belong to none of them. I did not exist as Frances's daughter, just as I never existed as Dana's sister.

I consider myself lucky in a way. My birth family brought me into their lives. Many adoptees are not that fortunate. Frances never lost touch with my birth father, Bobby, and she and his wife, Maureen, talked on a regular basis. When she traveled to Niagara Falls to visit family, she would also take time to see them. But in all the years and conversations, she never once mentioned me.

Two months after I found Frances, I wrote a letter to my birth father:

> *I've hesitated to write this letter, not really knowing how you felt about what happened 36 years ago. However, because you've kept in touch with my mother, Frances, I felt there might be a chance for us to develop some type of amicable relationship . . . Frances and I seem to be doing OK given the distance between us (we have outrageous telephone bills, though). I still don't know what she looks like, but she told me I look a lot like you . . . I've missed half my life with you. I'd really like to know you for the next half.*

When this letter from me arrived at my birth father's house, Maureen was thrilled. There was no hesitation. I was another daughter and she accepted me as such. It's been that way ever since. She's a wonderful woman who sees me as family.

My birth father, Bob, and his wife, Maureen.

My three sisters, though, took much longer to reach out to me. And that was okay; it was their decision. I was always willing to meet them, but the decision on whether I would be a part of their lives was completely up to them. They felt a keen loyalty to their mother, and it was difficult for them to embrace a sibling who was the result of one of their father's dalliances.

I am their blood, but we aren't the same. I wasn't a sister or daughter who moved away and came back into their lives. I never existed to any of them until 1996, even Frances, who held me for a fleeting moment as a tiny five-pound baby, her firstborn. I was there for an instant, and then I was gone.

My sisters and I try and see one another a couple of times a year. A few years back, we met for lunch to celebrate our birthdays since three of us have birthdays in September. They bought me gifts, and it made me feel so much like family. It was another watershed moment in my life.

A year before I found Frances, Mark recalled talking to our Aunt Mary Ann about my adoption. She told him that it was an event that traumatized Frances and that it fundamentally changed her. According to Mary Ann, Frances didn't want to give me up for adoption, but she had no choice.

I woke up at 1:30 A.M. the day of my sixty-first birthday, startled by a dream of a young woman giving up her baby for adoption. In that hazy half-awake state, I wondered not only whether Frances was in labor at 1:30 A.M. the day I was born, but who was with her.

A nurse? A social worker? Anyone? It's something I never asked. My thirty-six-year-old self didn't need to know, but my sixty-one-year-old self wished I would have found out so much more about my mother.

~⁂~

Birth is powerful, magical. Sheryl Feldman, author of *A Midwife's Story* and *Wise Birth*, believed that a woman is bestowed with a certain power when she gives birth, power passed from mother to child. I wonder if that is still true for a woman who relinquishes her child.

When I first met Frances, the veil of imagination was pulled away. She was flawed and restless, her joy always tempered by regret. And she often wanted what she couldn't have. She spent her life in love with Dana's father, but would she still have loved him if he was hers?

A big part of Frances died when Dana died, and I often wonder whether she wept over the fact that there would never be a photo with all of us in it, or a holiday with all of us together at the dinner table. Never in her life did she have the opportunity to be with her three children. That hole was impossible to fill.

Mark told me that he felt that I belonged to our family, and he never once considered me a stranger. "You and I are far more alike," Mark said of our relationship as siblings and of the family dynamic I would never experience. However, I found Dana in her words, and in those words, I discovered what joined her and me together. My brother, Mark, spent the first half of his life with her, but pointed out that soon he will have known me longer than the sister he grew up with.

The Dana that I would never know loved music. She loved to sing. She loved family. She loved to play board games and cards, and she loved to cook. She enjoyed comedies and acting. She was goofy. She could laugh at herself. She was sensitive.

She was a good sister to her younger brother. One Christmas she gave Mark a BMX magazine, and inside many of the pages were twenty-dollar bills.

At the end of every journal, Dana always summed up her life. When Mark was preparing to graduate and strike out on his own, she wrote about how close they were and hoped that he would survive the challenges ahead. When she spoke of Mom, she conceded: "*Again duality . . . fear and anger, bordering on hatred and also a very real love I'm a slave to. I see her trying harder than ever. If only I could make it alright for her. But I never could . . .*"

I carry the ghosts of loss; I look in the mirror for the person that may have been, a life that I could have had, and a family that was mine.

When I was in the orphanage, the nuns pinned a heart-shaped locket on me. It held religious medals and a small piece of paper folded neatly in a tiny square. When I was older, I patiently took it apart, hoping that the paper would tell me who I was. But it was just a prayer. The nuns sent me off to a new life with this talisman in the shape of a heart.

When I listened to the cassette tape with my mother's first words to me, I was taken back to those early days of our relationship, to a time when I felt as whole as I ever would. Not long after I played that tape, I wrote this:

June 29, 2021

From the chair on the porch I could see the fan rustling the calendar
  on the wall
in the kitchen.
It was in the mid 80s even though it was sunset.
The air was still, but I could sense a storm.
I heard your voice again tonight for the first time in years
and I almost believed
for a few seconds
that I could call you and ask about your weather.
It seemed like yesterday when we talked for hours on the phone,
when we lingered in the pasta aisle at the Tops supermarket in
  Niagara Falls at 1 A.M.,
when we ate pizza with everything, including anchovies,
when you opened a box of old photos and told me the stories behind
  each one.
It seemed like yesterday when you stood in the kitchen
of my old house
and we cooked together
and sang along with Andrea Bocelli.
I will never have you again,
your voice, floating in my dreams.
A reminder that I was yours but wasn't.
My arms, locking with yours as we strolled through an Ohio antiques
  market,
the arms that never had the chance to hold me nearly long enough.

CHAPTER 29

A GHOST COMES CALLING

September 10, 2022. Harvest moon. It was bright and gold and just touched by clouds at 6 A.M. For the first time in over a decade, I was traveling back to Dayton. It had been nearly three years since my mother's death.

I don't think I ever felt more of an orphan than during this final trip to the place my birth mom called home for the majority of her life. The lawyers for Frances's estate had pressed the courts to put the house on the market. She had spent considerable time in long-term care, and the state was seeking to recoup whatever costs possible. Mark's dad, Frank, nearly eighty-nine, still lived there. For how long, though, depended on how quickly the property sold. When that happened, he would have to find somewhere else to live.

The acreage was still walled in with trees and shrubs, shielding it from huge housing developments that now surrounded it. A for-sale sign was on the corner. This would be the final time I would pass through the door. The final time I would stand in Dana's room, the final time I would walk this small patch of land with my brother, Mark, and hear stories of his past, Dana's past.

My husband and I arrived a few minutes before Mark and his wife, Kerrie. I knocked on the screen door and said, "Hello, Frank!" and he called for us to come in. He was certainly frailer than the last time I visited, but he got around surprisingly well, and he still had a full head of wavy salt and pepper hair. I think he was delighted to have someone to talk to, and he asked about our lives and jobs and whether we were still playing music. I asked him about his health, and he showed me his medicine reminder box. It was filled with dozens of pills. He shrugged and said, "They keep me alive." It was Frank who insisted that I come back to Dayton and take some of my mother's things, and he was genuinely happy that I made the trip.

While looking around the house, it was easy to see that Frank had given up caring about it long ago. He had cleared himself space in the small living room with a recliner, love seat, and coffee table. Everything else was falling down around him, but what did it matter? Most likely he would be evicted as soon as someone put in a reasonable offer, and there was no doubt it would be leveled to make way for new development.

When Mark and Kerrie walked through the door, it seemed that no time had passed. It was as though we had seen one another just a few weeks ago. My brother and I hugged, the first time in probably a dozen years. Mark's curly dark hair was now flecked with gray, and he gave me a huge grin—he had our mother's smile. I felt a tinge of guilt that it had taken so long for us to reconnect, and for the reason we were all there: to sort through our mother's belongings before an excavator smashed the house to pieces.

Despite the easy familiarity Mark and I felt for one another, everything was different. The wreckage of my mother's life was all around me, stacked in piles on the dining room table, in boxes and bags, in dresser drawers, tucked away in closets, heaped on beds. It was as though someone had broken into the house and rummaged through every single thing to find whatever it was they were looking for. There was no rhyme or reason to any of it; it was complete chaos and it was overwhelming. In reality, it would take weeks to sort through my mother's belongings, and I had one day. I wondered whether Frances started the process of packing things in boxes and then got too sick to continue. Or was it Frank? At this point the reason didn't matter.

A couple of weeks before the trip, my brother said that he wanted Mom's KitchenAid mixer and a painting. I had given Frances a couple of cookbooks as Christmas gifts over the years, and I told Mark he should take them. His oldest son showed up later that afternoon. A budding chef, he carried a stack of cookbooks to his car.

Kerrie and I went through my mother's jewelry, most of it fun, quirky costume pieces, and I tried to imagine Frances wearing some of the big, bold necklaces and earrings. Kerrie was a collector of costume jewelry and was thrilled when I told her she should take it. I chose some necklaces, a couple of rings, and a small box of earrings, and I wished more than anything that Frances would have given me at least one piece when she was still alive.

Stacked on a dresser in Frances's room was a draft of an erotic novel she was writing, which was nothing more than a thinly veiled version of her life, as well as notebooks with sketches for this never-completed manuscript. There were a couple hundred pages, and I took them with me. Actually, I was glad it still existed. When she first started the project years ago, she sent me some pages to read, but the computer that I saved it on was long gone. Her family was appalled by this endeavor. I was in my mid-thirties when I found Frances, and that gave me a different perspective on her as a woman. She very much enjoyed the physical aspects of a relationship, and with her health failing, this may have been a way for her to relive that part of her life. I also found a journal from 2005, three months before Katrina and five months before Dana's body would be found during the hurricane cleanup. Frances carried a torch for Dana's father her entire life, and many of the entries expressed her ongoing love and devotion to him. "*How is it possible to love this deep?*" she wrote in early May 2005.

She and Dana's father would have a final falling out after the trial. According to Mark, Frances told him that he had "killed our daughter." Dana made her father promise to never tell Frances where she was living, and he kept that promise. Frances felt that if she had known Dana's whereabouts, she could have done something to help. Perhaps she could have even traveled to New Orleans and rescued her from the dead-end life she was living.

Dana's room was a catchall for even more boxes, dishes, clothes, and other junk. Squirrels had made nests in one corner, and one of the cubby holes had been boarded shut because they were chewing their way through the house. My heart was heavy at the state of this room I had slept in so many years ago. The beautiful quilt that was on the bed was horribly faded and torn and beyond saving. I was hoping that I would find the room as I remembered it, the quilt folded and stored somewhere safe, but nothing was the same. I closed my eyes and tried to recall Dana's words about the room. She mentioned its sagging yellow wallpaper and the oppressive summer heat. She must have sat on her bed and looked out its one window at the world outside, a world that she wanted to conquer.

Frances kept a locked trunk in her room, the contents of which had been a source of mystery for as long as Mark could remember. Mark and his oldest son carried it downstairs and placed it on the living room floor, and I couldn't help but think it was the same size and type of box that held Dana's body.

The view from Dana's window at her childhood home in Dayton

Frances could be a very secretive person, and the trunk could have contained anything, from a secret stash of cash to documents that revealed some unknown dark family history.

When Mark lifted the lid, the mystery was solved; it was filled with family photos. It wasn't what any of us expected, and Mark wondered why she would lock away something so benign, so joyous, as photos of her family. It should have been a thing to share with us when we were all together, not hidden under lock and key. These photos and other mementos would have given me so much more perspective and understanding of my birth family had I seen them twenty years ago. Among them were the letter and photos I sent Frances when I first discovered who she was.

Mark and I sat on the floor in front of the trunk and removed stacks of pictures. He had a story for nearly all of them—grandparents, aunts, uncles, cousins, and, of course, Mom and Dana. Frank was an excellent photographer, and there were some striking shots of Dana, Mark, and Frances. There were sweet photos of three-year-old Mark with a mop of dark curly hair. Dana must have enjoyed being photographed; she seemed a natural. There were photos of pensive Dana, precocious Dana, glamorous Dana. Our mother was beautiful and sassy and had a perfect smile. Frank recalled that her hair was dyed platinum blond when he first met her in California, and there were several photos of her with that blond hair teased high above her head. One in particular struck me: a photo of Frances from 1962, singing with a jazz band. Frances told me several times that she enjoyed singing, but I had no idea it was more than just a casual hobby. I don't know why she kept it all such a secret. Perhaps she looked back on her life and was disappointed in how it turned out, or perhaps she didn't want to be reminded of her past. Whatever the reason, she chose not to give us the opportunity to ask us any questions.

Throughout the day I had a nagging sense of unworthiness, as though I was barging in on another family. I felt awkward, and I most certainly felt like I was on the outside looking in. True, my brother and I shared a mother, and I was blood-related to just about everyone in every photo we looked at, but it is a history I wouldn't ever be able to experience. This was his life, and these were his people, and I silently and foolishly felt like an intruder.

Frances singing with a band, December 1962.

Before we left, Mark and I took some time to walk the grounds. For him, there were a lifetime of memories in the house and the acreage that surrounded it, and maybe the stroll was a way to say goodbye. So much had changed since his childhood.

He pointed up to a huge, old black walnut tree, heavy with walnuts nearly the size of tennis balls. "We had a tree house there," he said, and he remembered a violent lightning strike that split apart one of the oldest trees on the property. We walked further and he talked about the huge vegetable garden Mom grew each year. There was a bed for strawberries, berry bushes, apple and peach trees, and her beloved rose garden. All of it was gone, including the grape arbor. It had collapsed to the ground.

I wanted to see the house as it once was, perhaps cluttered but alive. I wanted to smell Frances's homemade bread and spaghetti sauce. I wanted to watch Mark outside, playing on the tire swing. I wanted to hear the laughter from friends who gathered there for summer barbecues, or Dana on the phone with one of her friends, whispering about boys.

Before the journals, I never even fathomed the questions that now consume me. Dana wrote of a family that I should have been a part of

The house in Dayton hidden by a magnificent black walnut tree.

but knew nothing about. My mother kept most of that world to herself. There is so much that I will never know. Mark said that Dana loved it there, and he was more than a little overwhelmed by the realization that he would also soon lose the place forever. My memories are few, but the time I spent with my mother in Dayton was always good. She tried so hard to make my visits fun and welcoming, and I was simply in awe that I had found my birth mother. At the time nothing else mattered. That was my focus more than anything else, and all the questions I now have—dredged up by reading Dana's journals—didn't exist then.

Frank swears that he still sees Frances in the house. Frances had often said that she saw Dana, that she could feel her presence. When the house is gone, where will these ghosts go? When the property is leveled and the trees cut down to make way for something new, when the barn and out-buildings are crushed and hauled away, who will remember these people? Will anyone tell the story of the young woman who looked out her bedroom window and dreamed of a grand and happy life, but instead would be found nearly nine hundred miles away, cut in pieces and stuffed in a particleboard trunk, and only discovered because of a hurricane? Would anyone know of the mother who gave away her firstborn? Would anyone understand the journey of that daughter and sister, standing alone in that same bedroom, looking out that same window and hopelessly wishing that it had all been different?

Is that my task, to write it all down so that it isn't forgotten? Whose story is it? Even now, I struggle to convince myself that I have presented a truer sense of my sister, a sister I never met, a sister who never once acknowledged my existence. But yet, here I am, knowing—absolutely certain—that she and I share so much that when I look in the mirror, I can see her.

I've asked my brother, Mark, whether he thinks Dana would have liked me. I still have a need to be accepted by her, and it still hurts that I never existed in the world of her journals. "I think she would have absolutely enjoyed your company," he said.

SEPTEMBER 2023 FULL CIRCLE

Another September, another journey. This time to Niagara Falls for my birth father's memorial service.

Twenty-seven years ago, I made my first trip to Niagara Falls, guided by written directions from Frances on how to reach my grandmother's house. I had dinner with my birth parents that evening, and I took a picture of them sitting together at our table. It was, conceivably, the perfect moment. They were genuinely happy, and I was the reason.

I stayed much too late and had to be at work the next day. My three-hour trip home was powered by adrenaline and an enormous amount of caffeine from one too many espressos.

My birth father had been hospitalized in 2023 after a bad fall early in the summer and died on July 6 at age eighty-nine. I had managed to visit him once, on July 1. "How do I look?" he said with a weak laugh when I walked into his hospital room. I knew he was near the end of his life; there was no mistaking it. He was retaining fluid, and his limbs were swollen to twice their normal size. His heart was failing, and he hadn't been able to leave his bed in nearly a month. He understood his grim state, but he also wanted to live. Perhaps more than anything, he didn't want this to be his ending. In a voice that was barely more than a whisper, he said that he wanted to go home because his biggest fear was dying in the hospital. This man, who at one time was enormously strong and fit, could barely move.

I thought back on my adoptive dad's last days. My birth father was surrounded by family and friends; my adoptive dad was completely

My birth parents, Bob and Frances.

alone. The memory sat uneasily in the pit of my stomach, and along with it was the ever-present guilt of not being a good daughter.

I'm not certain I was a good daughter to either father. I was perpetually absent from their lives, and even though my birth father's wife, Maureen, insisted that she understood because I lived 150 miles from them, had a full-time job and often had gigs on the weekends, I knew better. They were excuses. They were a way for me to stay just far enough away emotionally that I could sever the relationship without wrestling with the dreaded feeling of obligation.

Late in 2022, Maureen insisted that all of us get together at their house for the afternoon. She knew my father's health was failing, and she wanted to make sure that all his daughters had the opportunity to spend time with him.

We made plans to meet up on Veterans Day. I was off work, and I remember the weather being rainy but unseasonably warm. A week later, Niagara Falls was pummeled with four feet of snow.

We piled around him for photos, and he grumbled at the fuss we were making. Secretly, I knew he cherished having everyone there, and it was the last time we were all together. One of those photos was posted in a collage at the memorial service.

I have always had a measure of sadness over not learning more about his life. We talked nearly every Sunday for twenty-seven years but those conversations now seem terribly inadequate. Some evenings—especially in the winter—he would joke with me over my insistence to live in a place with four seasons. And he often reminded me that on the day he was born in early February 1934, Niagara Falls experienced its coldest temperature on record.

We talked about food a lot. My grandmother—"Ma," the patrons at the bar called her—was an incredible cook, and her pasta and meatballs were legendary. He liked the fact that I canned every summer and fall, just like she did. We always talked about music, and he never failed to ask me what gigs I had coming up. He struggled with bouts of depression, though, and during some of our phone calls, it was all I could do to get him to say anything positive. He often told me that he felt as though he was a failure, and the weight of his regrets was suffocating. Even into his eighties, I always thought there was more time. Time to unravel his life and get a glimpse of the mountainous bearded man and his ever-present cigar, smiling and happy as he tended bar and listened to some of the best jazz to be found anywhere in the state of New York.

Now I'm trying to hang on to the sound of his voice and his first words to me each week: "How are you, baby?"

My father's memorial service was a joyous celebration of remembrance, and each time someone stood up to speak, I learned something new about him, and how much he meant to so many of them.

I don't think my birth father ever got over the fact he had another daughter. Every time I saw him, he held my hands and touched my face and told me how much he loved me. I was an unexpected gift.

Perhaps it was the other way around. They were my gift.

The gift of family, no matter how broken.

The gift of knowledge, no matter how heartbreaking.

ACKNOWLEDGMENTS

I would like to thank Michele Nestor for all the support, input, and hours of discussion about my life and how my adoption shaped it, and for reading the initial rough drafts of the working document. She was never hesitant to tell me to keep pushing, that my life and my sister's words were inexplicably entwined, and that I needed to continue the journey.

A special thanks to John Ballance, director of photography for *The Advocate*, for his time and for permission to use the article that appeared in the *Times-Picayune*.

To Etta Dietz and Jill Golden, thank you both for reading and re-reading and suggesting and editing and being so open and honest with me.

I was fortunate to meet Jo Scheier, who writes under the pen name Patricia Thrushart, at a writers' meeting at the Watershed Book Shop in Brookville, Pennsylvania. She agreed to read an early version of the manuscript and continued to read ongoing edits of the project. Jo, thank you for your incredible insight and for pushing me forward to dig deeper and create a much more intimate narrative.

To say that I am very much indebted to professor and author Karen Weyant is an understatement. I am beyond grateful to her for spending so much time with the manuscript as I worked through it, reading it numerous times, editing it, and offering up so many outstanding comments to help me shape the direction of the project. Karen, I truly cannot ever thank you enough.

To my brother, Mark, for his encouragement and love and for sharing with me his memories of our mother and sister. This project could not have happened without you, little brother.

And to my husband, Mark, for being there from the very beginning.

Lastly, to Sunbury Press for seeing the potential in my manuscript and providing me with this incredible opportunity. I am both astonished and humbled, and I cannot thank you enough

ABOUT THE AUTHOR

REBECCA TITCHNER grew up in Bennetts Valley in Elk County, Pennsylvania. She is a graduate of St. Marys Area High School and holds a bachelor of science degree in Environmental Studies from Allegheny College.

For nearly a dozen years she was both a reporter and eventual editor of *The Ridgway Record* and *The Daily Press*. Since late 1999 she has been employed by Elk County as the county's Recycling Coordinator. In 2018 she was recipient of the Champion of the PA Wilds Conservation Stewardship award.

Titchner is a singer, musician, and songwriter. Her poetry and nonfiction have appeared in several regional literary journals. She resides in Ridgway with her husband, two dogs, and three very old cats.

www.ingramcontent.com/pod-product-compliance
Lightning Source LLC
Chambersburg PA
CBHW010728270326
41930CB00016B/3408